CRYPTO INVESTING GUIDE

The complete guide to investing in Cryptocurrencies, Bitcoin, Ethereum, Cardano, Solana, Learn how to trade them safely and with profit

Christian Hum

Copyright Christian Hum © 2022,

All rights reserved.

TABLE OF CONTENT

Introduction 4
Chapter 1: What are Cryptocurrencies? 25
Chapter 2: Players in Cryptocurrencies 42
Chapter 3: Classification of Cryptocurrencies 53
Chapter 4: Investing in Cryptocurrency 184
Conclusion 194

Introduction

Blockchain is a secure transaction ledger database (initially made to facilitate currency exchanges) shared by all the members participating in an established, distributed network of computers. Blockchain is a type or subset of what is called ledger technology ("DLT") technology. DLT is a way to record and share data in all data centers (also known as ledgers), one by one, have precisely the same data records and are shared together and managed for distribution by a network of computer servers, called nodes. Blockchain is an encryption machine known as cryptography and uses (a set of) specific mathematical algorithms to create and ensure the formation of continuously growing data, when data can only be added and when existing data cannot be deleted, that takes a type of "trade barriers", which acts as a distributed block. Infact, blockchain is a technology with many faces. It can show different features and occupy a comprehensive program of programs ranging from fully open and unrestricted to accredited.

In an open, unauthorized blockchain, a person can join or leave the network at will, without exception or must (before) be approved by any (middle) organization. All that is required to join a network once to add activity to a book is a computer in which the appropriate software is installed. There is no middle owner of the network and the software, and the same copies of the ladder are the same and are distributed across all nodes in the network. Most confidential funds currently exist of the rotation is based on unauthorized blockchains (e.g. Bitcoin, Bitcoin Cash, Litecoin).

In an approved blockchain, transaction verifications (i.e. nodes) must be pre-selected by network administrator (who sets the rules of the client) to be able to join the network. This allows, among other things, to easily verify the identity of network participants. However, in time at the same time it also requires network participants to put their trust in the central integration company in order to select reliable network nodes.In general, permissioned blockchains can be further divided into two subcategories. On the one hand, there are open or public permissioned blockchains, which can be accessed and viewed by anyone, but where only authorised network participants can generate transactions and/or update the state of the ledger.

On the other hand, there are closed or "enterprise" permissioned blockchains, where access is restricted and where only the network administrator can generate transactions and update the state of the ledger. What is important to note is that just like on an open permissionless blockchain, transactions on an open permissioned blockchain can be validated and executed without the intermediation of a trusted third-party. Some cryptocurrencies, like Ripple and NEO utilise public permissioned blockchains.

Cryptocurrencies.

Blockchain technology is said to be as disruptive as The Internet. White paper, by Satoshi Nakamoto (pseudonym), "Bitcoin: The Peer-to-Peer Electronic Cash System" appeared in 2008, to put everything in motion. White paper describes it as electronic cash transactions are possible between peers without the need for a third party group (financial institution). Since then, the paper has been quoted in 5,687 times at the time of writing this introduction. Digital signatures and cryptography will be used to protect financial transactions, and peers in the bitcoin network operating on blockchain technology will ensure, confirm and authorize efforts to eliminate "double expenditure problem".

According to Nakamoto (2008), this will make the system and work transparent, consistent and subject to peer pressure, thereby eliminating the need for financial institutions and their costly costs. Bitcoin the network will set the time stamp for the action to accelerate further action a series of hash-based work evidence, forming an unchangeable record without renewing the proof of employment. A very long chain will not work as well evidence of the sequence of events in which it was proved, but evidence that it came from a large CPU power pool. Messages are broadcast with the best effort, and nodes can leave and join the network at will, receiving the most remote a chain of evidence of work as proof of what happened while they were gone.

The website BlockGeeks.Com (2019) defines "blockchain" as a growing list of records, called blocks, is connected using cryptography. Each block contains a cryptographic hash of the previous block, a time stamp and synthetic data (usually represented as a Merkle tree). By design, the blockchain resists data conversion. It is "an open, wide ledger that can record transactions between two parties effectively and efficiently and permanently". Use of Blockchain with peer-to-peer electronic money transactions enabled the Finance number Technology (FinTech) applications, Distributed Ledger Technology (DLT) applications and submissions to more than a thousand others Cryptocurrencies.

Bitcoin remains the most popular cryptocurrency. Blockchains have now shifted from electronic money to other government programs, supply chain management, health care, agriculture, wealth, international development and almost any such application use secure data that can be changed to secure, unencrypted, A website based on consensus, transparency and trust. Apart from FinTech applications, other blockchains-based applications are emerging in all sectors and industries as everyone aims to benefit of the special blockchains structures mentioned in the previous sentence. After the success or failure of bitcoin (depending), people try apply it to practices and processes beyond financing.

Some examples of real-world blockchain applications in use are as follows:

- Land Ownership and Management: Dubai, USA, UK, Sweden, Ukraine, Georgia and Ghana.

- Development Aid: Aid Transfer Efficiency, South African Early Childhood Development.

- Supply Chain Management: Diamond Tracking (De Beers), Food Safety (Walmart), Oil Supply (ADNOC), Agricultural Products Supply (LDC).

- Renewable Energy: WePower (Estonia), Power Ledger (Australia), Acciona Energy (Spain), The Brooklyn Micro Grid (US), The Sun Exchange (South Africa).

- Remittances: Blockchain Wallet, TransferWise, Ripple's XRP, BitSpark, MoneyFi, Chynge.

- Digital Identity: Civic, ValidatedID, THEKEY, Trusti, PeerMountain, Edge, BlockAuth, BlockVerify, CryptID, ExistenceID. ·

- Agriculture: Food Traceability, Fair Trade Farming, Organic Farming Certifications, Food Safety (Pesticides Use), New Markets, Logistics. ·

- Democracy and Governance: Voting, Decentralisation of Services, GovCoin,

Democracy.Earth, FollowMyVote, Smart Participation, Liquid Democracy. ·

- Manufacturing and Industrial: Provenance, JioCoin, Hijro, SKUChain, BlockVerify, STORJ.io, RFID Integration, Anti Counterfeiting, Compliance. ·

- Health: Modum.io, Gem, SimplyVital Health, MedRec, Electronic Health Records (EHR), Ambr0Sys, Hashed Health, Medical Change, Change Health. ·

- Financial Inclusion: MojaLoop, ABRA, Bank Apoalim, Maersk, Augur, Regalii, Ripple, World Remit, Stellar, Oridian, Credits.Vision, OneName, ShoCard. ·

- Retail: OpenBazaar, Loyyal, Blockpoint.io, Customer Data Management, Transparency, Warranty, Goods Tracking, Customer Loyalty.

- Climate Change: Power Ledger, ClimateCoin.io, Carbon Emission Trading, Clean Energy, GHG.

- · Environment: SOLshare, PlasticBank, Agora Tech Lab, EnergiToken, CarbonX, Veridium, IBM, United Nations, Waste Reduction, GiveTrack.

- Human Rights: Stop the Traffik, Dash Venezuela, Micro Trade, OpenGarden, RightMesh, Media Freedom, Social Media Awareness.

- Access to Water: Clean Water Coin, Decentralized Water Management, Water Quality Assurance Regulations, Water Trading.

- Cyber-security: GuardTime, REMME, IoT Security, Decentralized Storage Solutions, Safer DNS, Security in P2P Messaging systems.

How a blockchain works: the basics

a. The blockchain is a distributed database: In simple terms, the blockchain can be thought of as a distributed database. Additions to this database are initiated by one of the members (i.e. the network nodes), who creates a new "block" of data, which can contain all sorts of information. This new block is then broadcasted to every party in the network in an encrypted form (utilising cryptography) so that the transaction details are not made public. Those in the network (i.e. the other network nodes) collectively determine the block's validity in accordance with a pre-defined algorithmic validation method, commonly referred to as a "consensus mechanism". Once validated, the new "block" is added to the blockchain, which essentially results in an update of the transaction ledger that is distributed across the network. In principle, this mechanism can be used for any kind of value transaction and can be applied to any asset that can be represented in a digital form.

b. Active "Blocks" are signed with a digital signature using a secret key: Every user on the blockchain network has a set of two keys. A secret key, used to build a digital signature transaction, as well as public key, known to everyone on the network. A public key has two uses: 1) it acts as an address on the blockchain network; and 2) is used for verification digital signature / verifies the sender. In the Bitcoin blockchain, this translates into the following example. Suppose Anna wants it send 100 Bitcoins to Jeff, and then first he will have to sign this purchase using his secret key (only known to him). He will have to talk about transactions in Jeff's public key, which is Jeff's address on the Bitcoin network.

Next, the action, which will be collected in a "transaction block", will need to be verified by nodes within the Bitcoin network. This is Anna's place a public key will be used to verify his or her signature. If Anna's signature is valid, the network will process the file transaction, add a block to the chain and transfer 100 Bitcoins from Anna to Jeff. Public and private user keys are stored in a digital wallet or e-wallet. Such a bag can be stored either stored online (Internet storage is often referred to as "hot storage") and / or offline (storage is offline commonly referred to as "cold storage").

c. No involvement of middleman: One of the key advantages of blockchain technology is that it allows for the simplification of many functions that usually require external company mediation (e.g. caregiver, bank, mortgage payment system, broker dealers, trading archive). In fact, blockchain is about extending trust and making decentralized authentication transaction. Simply put, it allows cutting "middle man". In many cases this will result in better performance. However, it is important to emphasize that it may also expose the co-parties to certain risks that were previously controlled by these mediators. For example, the Bank for International Settlements ("BIS") recently warned in a report of 2017 entitled Distributed ledger technology in payment, cleaning and payment, that approval blockchain technology may introduce new financial risks. Much generally seems when the functions of the mediator as a deterrent to significant risks, such as systemic risk, can simply not be so replaced by blockchain technology.

Blockchain compatibility methods

In fact, any node within a blockchain network can suggest the addition of new information to blockchain. To ensure this is a supplement to information (for example a function record) is valid; nodes must reach some kind of agreement. Here "harmony the machine" enters. In short, the consensus approach is a pre-defined goal (cryptographic) authentication method that verifies the correct sequence of transactions in blockchain. In the case of cryptocurrencies, such a sequence is necessary to address the problem of "Double spending" (i.e. the issue that one instrument or asset may have transfers more than once if the transfer is unregistered and managed in the center).

The consensus approach can be organized in many ways. After that, two of the best known and in the context of cryptocurrencies are also the most commonly used - consensus examples are Methods to be briefly discussed: Proof of Work ("PoW") and Proof of Stake ("PoS") method.

a. Proof of Work (PoW): In the PoW program, network participants have to solve so-called "cryptographic puzzles" to allow adding new "blocks" to the blockchain. This paradoxical process is often called "mines". In simple terms, these cryptographic mysteries have been created with all the information before recorded on the blockchain and a new transaction set to be added to the next "block".Because the input of each compound becomes larger over time (resulting in a complex calculation), PoW the machine requires a large number of computer resources, which consume a significant amount of this electricity. When a network participant (i.e. a node) solves a cryptographic puzzle, it proves that you are done with the work, and is rewarded with a digital value proposition (or in the case of a cryptocurrency, recently acquired coin in the mine). This award serves as an incentive for network support. The cryptocurrency Bitcoin is based on the PoW consensus approach. Other examples include Litecoin, Bitcoin Cash, Monero, etc.

b. Proof of Stake (PoS): In a PoS system, a verifier of action (i.e. network location) must verify ownership of a particular asset, (or in the case of cryptocurrencies, a certain number of coins) to participate in the verification transactions. This transaction verification transaction is called a "forging" instead of a "mine". Because for example, in the case of cryptocurrencies, a transaction guarantor will have to prove his or her "stake" (i.e. his / her own share) of all available coins to be allowed verifying activity. Depending on how much money you have hold on, you will have a higher chance of being the one to secure the next block (i.e., all of this has to be done and that he has a large size within the network that earns him the most trusted position) .

Activity guarantor is paid for transaction by its performance assurance services groups.

Cryptocurrencies like Neo and Ada (Cardano) use the PoS compatibility method.

c. Alternatives mechanisms

PoW and PoS methods are far removed from existing consensus procedures. Other examples include proof of performance, proof of elapsed time and proof of capacity. Other analysis of these methods falls outside the scope of this study.

Blockchain technology can have many applications

Although blockchain technology is often associated with digital or virtual currency schemes, payments and financial services, the scope is enormous. Blockchain can obviously be used in large area different sectors (e.g. trade and commerce, health care, administration). Moreover, it has been many possible applications. It can affect the security of the collateral, to registration of shares, bonds and other assets, in the transfer of property ties, in the operation of land registers, etc. Analysis of these applications falls outside this study. As pointed out above, this study will only touch upon the subject of blockchain technology where this is meaningful for the research on cryptocurrencies and can be deemed relevant from the perspective of combating money laundering, terrorist financing and/or tax evasion.

Chapter One
What are Cryptocurruencies?

Cryptocurrencies are virtual currencies with no physical form that operate on a peer-to-peer basis without a central authority. They are digital and, unlike the US dollar, they have no physical form and no central repository. The decentralized nature of cryptocurrencies requires computers to use cryptography, computerized encoding and decoding of information to verify transactions and prevent counterfeiting.

Unlike traditional currencies, which use a trusted third party such as a credit card company or bank to verify that the funds are available to complete a transaction, cryptocurrencies rely on a network of computers to confirm the transaction and that the spender has the coins to transfer. When a transaction is initiated, it is broadcast to the network where it awaits verification from computers that solve an algorithm to determine if the transaction is legitimate. Establishing a definition of hidden funds is not an easy task. It's like blockchain, cryptocurrencies, it has become the term "buzzword" to refer to the various technological advances it uses a process better known as cryptography. In simple terms, cryptography is a way to do it protect information by converting it (i.e. encrypting it) into an unreadable readable format specified (or encrypted) by a person with a secret key. Confidential funds such as Bitcoin, protected in this way using an intelligent system of public and private digital keys. Following this we attempt to provide an appropriate definition of crypto currencies on the basis of critical analysis descriptions already made by various relevant policy makers in Europe and abroad level.

Cryptocurrencies are "digital money" that do not physically exist but can be converted to any popular physical currency. Bitcoin, the first digital money, was hatched as an act of defiance. Unleashed in the wake of the Great Recession, the cryptocurrency was touted by its early champions as an antidote to the inequities and corruption of the traditional financial system. Bitcoin sought to replace the services provided by financial institutions with cryptography and code. When you pay your mortgage, a series of agreements occur in the background between your financial institution and others, enabling money to go from your account to someone else's. Bitcoin and other cryptocurrencies replace those background agreements and transactions with software — specifically, a distributed and secure database called a Blockchain. If you could piece together a running tabulation of who held every dollar, then suddenly the physical representations would become unnecessary.

Bitcoin achieved the running tabulation by creating a single, universally accessible digital ledger called a blockchain. Bitcoin's blockchain, unlike the ledgers maintained by traditional financial institutions, is replicated on networked computers around the globe and is accessible to anyone with a computer and an Internet connection. A class of participants on this network, called miners, is responsible for detecting transaction requests from users, aggregating them, validating them and adding them to the blockchain as new blocks. It's called a chain because changes can be made only by adding new information to the end. Each new addition, or block, contains a set of new transactions — a couple of thousand that reference previous transactions in the chain.

1. Policy makers: ECB, IMF, BIS, EBA, ESMA, World Bank and FATF

Since the emergence of Bitcoin in 2009, the topic of cryptocurrencies has been under consideration different policy makers, each of whom touched on a topic in a different way.

a. ECB

The European Central Bank ("ECB") has classified cryptocurrencies as part of its monetary policy. In the 2012 Virtual Currency Scheme Report described those currencies as uncontrolled digital money, usually issued and controlled by its developers, and used and accepted among members of a particular virtual community. It also clarified that the three types of tangible currencies can be classified depending on working with traditional currencies and the real economy:

i. virtual currency that can only be used in a closed virtual system, usually in online games (e.g. Gold World Gold);

ii. Tangible investments linked unilaterally to the real economy: the conversion rate exists. Buy the currency (in traditional currency) and the purchase price can follow used for purchasing tangible goods and services (and specifically for purchasing real goods as well services) e.g. Facebook accounts.

iii. Virtual currency connected twice in real economy: there are conversion rates both to buy cash that is as good as selling that money; purchased money can used to purchase both tangible assets such as real goods and services.

Cryptocurrencies, like Bitcoin, are coins of the latest version: they can both be purchased in traditional currency as sold in traditional currency, and can be used to purchase both digital and real goods and services. In a recent 2015 report entitled Virtual Currency Schemes - further analysis, the ECB has prioritized a "second", and most updated definition of tangible funds. Define tangible currency as digital valuable submissions, which may be issued by the central bank, credit bureau or e-money center, which in some cases it can be used as an alternative to money. It also clarified that cryptocurrencies, like Bitcoin, it creates a decentralized bi-directional currency (i.e. two countries).

b. IMF

Like the ECB, the International Monetary Fund ("IMF") has classified cryptocurrencies as subset real money, which he describes as digital value propositions, issued by independent engineers once included in its account unit. According to the IMF, the concept of real money covers a wide range of 'currencies', from simple IOUs ("Informal credit certificates" or "I owe you ") by issuers (such as Internet or mobile coupons and flight miles), tangible funds are supported commodities like gold, and cryptocurrencies like Bitcoin.

c. BIS

Market Payments and Market Infrastructure Committee ("CPMI"), International Bank body, Settlements ("BIS"), has cryptocurrencies eligible as digital currencies or digital currency schemes. These programs are said to reflect the following important features:

i. They are assets, the amount of which is determined by supply and demand, similar in concept goods like gold, but of zero value;

ii. Use distributed levers to allow electronic peer-to-peer exchanges an amount where there is no trust between the parties and without the need for mediators; and

iii. They are not used by any person or institution.

d. EBA

The European Banking Authority ("EBA") has recommended that cryptocurrencies be referred to as virtual financial, which defines61 as a digital representation of value that can be generated by a domain a bank or public authority or attached to fiat money but used naturally or legally people as a means of exchange and can be transferred, stored or traded electronically.62

e. ESMA

The European Securities and Markets Authority ("ESMA") also recently mentioned it cryptocurrencies as tangible currencies, is a pan-European warning issued in conjunction with European Insurance and Occupational Pension Authority ("EIOPA") and EBA.63 Fully definition of EBA, virtual currency is defined as the digital expression of a non-single value issued or certified by a central bank or public authority and does not have the legal status of money or money.

f. World Bank

The World Bank has classified cryptocurrencies as part of digital currencies, which it explains digital value propositions are included in their account unit, which are separate from the currency, which is simply a digital payment method, represented and deposited with fiat money. Contrary to many other policy makers, the World Bank also described cryptocurrencies itself as digital currencies that rely on cryptographic techniques to achieve consistency.

g. FATF

Like many other policy makers, the Financial Action Task Force ("FATF") is fast approaching cryptocurrensets as a subset of virtual currency, defining it as a digital expression of value which can be digitally traded and act (1) as a means of trade; and / or (2) an account unit; and / or (3) a value store, but does not have the legal tender status (i.e., when awarded to a lender, is an agreement legal and legal payment) anywhere. It also suggests that tangible funds can be divided into two basic types:

i. Flexible currencies that have the same amount of real and potential currency traded back and forth for real money; these virtual investments can be of a single or a state of segregation (i.e. they may have centralized authority for that controls the system with or without central monitoring); and

ii. Fixed amounts of fixed currencies specific to a specific domain or world (e.g. Multiplayer Role Play online (World of Warcraft), and under the rules governs its use, it cannot be exchanged for fiat money. Cryptocurrencies like Bitcoin are virtual currencies of the first type, which can, according to the FATF, be defined as math-based, decentralized convertible virtual currencies that are protected by cryptography.

Cryptocurrencies - Tokens - Cryptosecurities

The term cryptocurrencies is often used incorrectly in a very broad sense. It will be so shown below, should be separated from both tokens and cryptosecurities.

a. Cryptocurrencies - Tokens

First, crypto currency should be separated from cryptographic "tokens", which provide a working outside of and beyond the normal purpose of trading. Tokens are issued in the framework of the First Token Offering or "ITO" to raise funds for a specific project or business. They form a novel class of crypto-assets (i.e., digital assets recorded in a distributed environment a letter, protected by cryptography) covering a particular type of claim against (or against the business) cash flow, assets, residual value, future assets or services, ...) arising from blockchain use technology.

Some tokens are similar to traditional instruments such as shares or bonds and are often called by them "As security tokens" or "investment tokens". Some tokens give their owners (future) access to certain products or services and are often referred to as "utility tokens". They can be used obtain certain products or services; however they do not serve the general purpose exchange, simply because they can usually be used only in place of the token itself.

b. Cryptocurrencies - Cryptosecurities

Second, cryptocurrencies should be separated from the new concept the so-called "cryptosecurities". In short, it has been argued that blockchain technology can also used to register issue and transfer ordinary shares and other securities of companies, in order to make the company capital table always accurate and up-to-date. Because this technology the process will be protected by cryptography, it has been suggested that these securities be defined as cryptosecurities. The only connection between these newly developed concepts is "cryptosecurities" and cryptocurrencies, that they both use blockchain technology.

Cryptocurrencies - Blockchain

Cryptocurrencies and blockchain have become hot topics for the past few years. While both are often referred to in the same sentence and are clearly connected, one should never mistake one another. Blockchain is a type of distributed ledger technology that builds the backbone of the crypto-market. Technology that supports a wide variety of cryptocurrencies currently is available. Its scope and field of use, however, are not limited to that. As stated above, the blockchain can be used in a variety of fields and can have a wide range of applications. Icon it is important to draw a clear line between these applications and cryptocurrencies, just one more direct use of blockchain technology. Against this background, administrators need not fear to prevent new inventions when addressing the issue of cryptocurrencies.

Chapter Two
Players in cryptocurrency

The cryptocurrency market is a new gaming platform where different actors each play a specific role. To give more light on how the market works, and without trying to get it all over, we will do it after this go on to identify key players.

1. Cryptocurrency users

The first, and most important, player is the "cryptocurrency user". The cryptocurrency user is natural a person or legal entity that obtains coins to use (i) to purchase real or genuine goods or services (from a set of specific vendors), (ii) making P2P payments, or (iii) holding to invest objectives (i.e.

speculative) . Without trying to eliminate everything, a cryptocurrency user can earn his or her coins in many ways:

• First, they can simply buy coins in the cryptocurrency market using fiat or other currencies cryptocurrency;

• Second, he can buy his coins directly from another cryptocurrency user (i.e. by trading stage - this exchange form is often referred to as "P2P exchange");

• Thirdly, if cryptocurrency is based on the PoW consensus approach, it can dig up a new coin (i.e. participate in verifying transactions by solving the "cryptographic puzzle" and be rewarded new coin);

• Fourth, in some cases he can get his coins directly from the moneylender, or as part of the first free coin offering (e.g. on the Stellar Lumens Network (XLM) is offered free) or in the framework of a crowd auction organized by a fundraiser (e.g. bulk of ether (e.g. Ethereum) was sold at a public auction to cover certain development costs);

• Fifth, if he sells goods or services in exchange for cryptocurrency, he may also receive coins such as payment for those goods or services;

• Sixth, in the event of a "strong fork" 84 blockchain coin, you will automatically receive the amount newly formed coin; and

• Finally, they can receive coins as a gift or donation from another cryptocurrency user.

2. Miners

A second player is the "miner" who participates in validating transactions on the blockchain by solving a "cryptographic puzzle". As explained above, the process of mining relates to cryptocurrencies that are based on a PoW consensus mechanism. A miner supports the network by harnessing computing power to validate transactions and is rewarded with newly mined coins (i.e. through an automatic decentralized new issuance). Miners can be cryptocurrency users, or, more commonly, parties who have made a new business out of mining coins to sell them for fiat currency (such as US dollar or Euro) or for other cryptocurrencies. Some miners group in so-called pools of miners to bundle computing power. At present, the risks associated with so-called "mining businesses" appear to be underestimated. We will further elaborate on this below.

3. Cryptocurrency exchanges

A third group of key players are the so-called "cryptocurrency exchanges". Cryptocurrency exchanges are persons or entities who offer exchange services to cryptocurrency users, usually against payment of a certain fee (i.e. a commission). They allow cryptocurrency users to sell their coins for fiat currency or buy new coins with fiat currency. They usually function both as a bourse and as a form of exchange office. Examples of well-known cryptocurrency exchanges are: Bitfinex[91], HitBTC, Kraken and Coinbase GDAX. It is important to note that some exchanges are pure cryptocurrency exchanges, which means that they only accept payments in other cryptocurrencies, usually Bitcoin (for example Binance), whilst others also accept payments in fiat currencies such as US dollar or Euro (for example Coinbase).

Furthermore, many cryptocurrency exchanges only allow their users to buy a particular selection of coins. It should also be noted that many cryptocurrency exchanges (i.e. both regular and pure cryptocurrency exchanges) operate as custodian wallet providers[97] (for example Bitfinex). In general cryptocurrency exchanges offer their users a wide array of payment options, such as wire transfers, PayPal transfers, credit cards and other coins. Some cryptocurrency exchanges also provide statistics on the cryptocurrency market (like trading volumes and volatility of the coins traded) and offer conversion services to merchants who accept payments in cryptocurrencies.

4. Trading Platform

In addition to cryptocurrency trading, so-called "trading platforms" also play an important role cryptocurrency exchanges (and, in particular, allow cryptocurrency users to purchase coins or money). Marketplace trading platforms that include different cryptocurrency users are available or if they want to buy or sell coins, they provide a platform where they can trade directly with each other (i.e. "eBay" for cryptocurrencies). Trading platforms are sometimes called "P2P trading" or "limited exchange". They are different from cryptocurrency trading in many ways. First and foremost, consumers or sell them for coins. Secondly, they are not owned by the governing body or company that takes charge and processes all trading activities, but only software (i.e., no central point authority). Trading platforms simply connect buyer and seller, allowing him to enter into an agreement, online, or in a personal place (i.e. face-to-face trading, usually done in cash). A well-known example of a Bitcoins trading platform is LocalBitcoins.

5. Wallet providers

Another group of key players are the so-called "fund providers". Wallet providers are those businesses providing cryptocurrency users with digital wallets or e-wallets used for holding, storing and to transfer coins. Simply put, a wallet holds the cryptographic keys of a cryptocurrency user. The wallet provider typically translates cryptocurrency activity history easily readable format, which looks like a normal bank account. In fact, there are several types of fund providers:

• Hardware wallet providers who provide cryptocurrency users with specific hardware solutions keep cryptographic keys private (e.g. Ledger Wallet).

• Software wallet providers who provide cryptocurrency users with software applications allow them to access the network send and receive coins and store cryptographic in your area keys (e.g. Jaxx).

• Wallet providers in charge (online) of cryptographic keys for cryptocurrency user (e.g. Coinbase).

6. Money Makers

There are also those so-called "money makers". Money makers are individuals either organizations that have developed cryptocurrency technology foundations and laid the foundation rules for its use. In some cases their ownership is known (e.g. Ripple, Litecoin, Cardano), but still they usually remain anonymous (e.g. Bitcoin, Monero). Some are still involved in care once developing cryptocurrency code and a basic algorithm (basically without a controller power), while others simply disappear (e.g. Bitcoin).

7.   Providers of funds

The last group of key players will be distinguished by "coin donors". Coin providers are individuals or organizations that provide coins to cryptocurrency users on initial coin issuance, or against payment (i.e. in crowdsale) with or without charge (i.e., in a specific framework (registration), System (e.g. Stellar - see below)), usually to support coin development or enlargement thunder. Coins offered by these coin providers to cryptocurrency users are created or mined before the coin official issuance / coin launch. Coins distributed in this way may be partially mined or pre-created (i.e., cryptocurrency users can still generate more coins after issuance), or they are complete previously excavated or previously created. In the latter case the issuer of the coin usually saves a large portion of the coins (e.g. this is the case with Stellar).

It is important to note that not all coins have a designated currency provider, and not all coins are pre-mined or whether its full supply was created in advance. A donor can be the same person as the founder of a fund, or another person or organization.

Chapter Three
Classification of cryptocurrencies

Before making decisions about the relevant regulations and application of cryptocurrency, it is important that the first domain about it technical performance is understood. The development of cryptocurrency is happening with new techniques in the field of cryptography. Digital Encryption Standard (DES), the latest major breakthrough in the field of cryptography, began in the early 1970's (Leech and Chinworth, 2001). DES operated by locking the code with the key. If the code reads 1-2-3-4 and the key was 2, the code can be pressed into 2-4-6-8. In this way, the code encrypted in the DES method it will be difficult to extract it without the knowledge of key.

Blight (2013) explained that the conflict arose in relation to DES in a similar way in the controversy surrounding the technology behind cryptocurrency today. It was said DES encryption could prevent public safety officials from entering determining the content of the software. If software content can be harmful was misunderstood, then risks would be imposed on the United States.

Blight goes describing the efforts made by the various groups to improve DES and create a system a key that was not readily available as used the popular 56-bit DES. This because, as Blight concludes, computer power is advanced until the solution encrypted code constructed in this way may be forcibly enforced. The development of these groups is built on a cryptocurrency concept system developed by Brands (1994). In this program, Brands describes how powerful computing is power that was not available at the time of his writing was able to make the system more efficient which code transfer was protected. It is therefore reasonable to assume that Brands helped pioneer the idea of a protected transfer of a group of others, today known as blockchain.

The creative use of the blockchain can be seen today in other applications such as transfer of title deeds or medical records. The modern method of encryption involves the use of single hash algorithms. Like DES, hash algorithms use input values to encrypt. Because for example, if the input value is 600 and the hashing algorithm is 50, the hash value says 30,000. Unlike DES, hash algorithms use two different values, one value for encryption and the single value that will be encrypted (Konheim, 2010). Because of this, one information key will not allow the person access to encrypted information. Additionally, hash algorithms go far beyond any variations that DES may have. Hash value can use 128-bit numbers represented by $2 \wedge 128$. As a result, data encrypted with hash algorithms resists aggression (Konheim, 2010.)

Abramowicz (2014) explained that current technology is powerful cryptocurrency is a blockchain. The following information is based on the texts of Abramowicz (2014). The blockchain works by creating a series for all users agree on the transaction that is taking place. Whenever a user does not agree that the function is so active, they were kicked in the chain and a fork formed. The fork doesn't help at all one user is a member but if enough users decide to break, a different chain is created and the two chains cannot communicate with each other. The purpose of the blockchain is to make sure all transactions are legal. This technology includes that all members of the blockchain is known and the values associated with each member are unknown. Drawing can be helpful to fully understand the function of blockchain sales. For example, if John wants to pay Bill for ten coins in blockchain, John will need to know Bill blockchain address. Then he sang a series of incredibly mathematical operations to encrypt and send them blockchain to Bill's address. Although Bill has already received the coins, he cannot send them to another group. This is because the Bill must wait for other members of the Council blockchain to verify transactions. The bill does not need to wait for all members to ratify transaction; you only need to wait for the particular team he is sending to funds to ensure work.

However, blockchain encryption and authentication process cost both goals of power and time. For example, according to Digicominist (2019), it needs more than 2.5 times more electricity to process a single Bitcoin transaction as it does in 100,000 Visa transactions. The Digicominist report goes on to explain that the power of the year use of all bitcoin transactions accounts for more than 1% of the United States total power consumption. Apart from this, cryptocurrency transactions are usually much faster than those standard digital transactions. Visa transactions, for example, can take one to three days process. However, Bitcoin transactions are possible for less than 30 minutes. Speed and encryption of cryptocurrency trading has made the blockchain the preferred method use of cryptocurrency. Additionally, attempts to balance between energy costs and time have resulted different ways to generate cryptocurrency. For example, XRP, second the most popular cryptocurrency after Bitcoin, has introduced ways to reduce costs and increase transaction speed (Kaustav, 2018).

Kaustav goes on to explain that this development was brought about by the development of technology used in creation blockchain. Similarly, as Kaustav pointed out, some cryptocurrencies have it appears over time and clicks for faster speeds and lower costs. However, Kaustav notes, as XRP users, use the most effective financial authority to discard existing ones the user base of the most popular coins. It is the continuation of innovation in the field of cryptocurrency and the desire to live in domains with a large population cryptocurrencies have existed and will continue to exist.

It is important from an auditor's perspective to understand the motive behind the use of multiple cryptocurrencies and available technologies. This understanding enables the auditor to ask appropriate questions of the detainee cryptocurrency and help detect errors or fraud. Public Company Accounting the Oversight Board (PCAOB) has issued auditors' guidance on dealing with clients. This guidance can be issued and applied to cryptocurrency. For example, if the auditor does not realize that all blockchain members can know the amount of coins stored in it address, then he may not ask the employee in charge of the cryptocurrency the address of the report confirming the amount provided to the fund from other members blockchain. If the auditor fails to do so, he or she will not be able to issue a valid audit ideas related to the existence and cryptocurrency rating of the tested company account.

In a situation where company executives are unable to provide a reassuring report the accuracy of their cryptocurrency account, the auditor can begin to become independent investigation using a blockchain tester. Kuzono and Karam (2017) explained that this is a tool that acts as a blockchain member and can search blockchain addresses. They also explained that if the auditor knew the blockchain address, he can use a blockchain tester to view all transactions that take place on it iketango. This purchase can be used to ensure the accuracy of the record transactions around the company's cryptocurrency account.

Government Cryptocurrency Law

Considering the technological power that operates after the development of cryptocurrency, government regulators can make judgments based on the results that cryptocurrency has on crime and the economy. The positive and negative effects that were carrying cryptocurrency will be analyzed to determine the appropriate policy. However, before the cryptocurrency pros and cons, existing policy should be reviewed in relation to similar regulated items. For example, a financial tool very similar to cryptocurrency can be securities that are traded publicly. The prices of both items can be easily determined by looking at the latest sale price. Additionally, securities and cryptocurrency are digitally traded and involved safety features to prevent their transfer between the parties. Finally, both items are often traded with expatriate groups for expansion the complexity of the policy aimed at controlling domestic use. Like as a result of this similarity, it is wise to look at the rules governing trade securities to determine which principles apply to cryptocurrency. One of the biggest rules separating stock sold publicly the stock traded in secret is a requirement to disclose detailed financial information about company operations.

The Sarbanes-Oxley Act of 2002 amplified this and required several regulations that would ensure reliability present financial information (Congress.gov, 2002). This disclosure is required domestic and foreign companies traded on the U.S. stock exchange. For now, cryptocurrency creators are not required to disclose anything publicly information about the development of their cryptocurrency, or related statistics future corporate cryptocurrency plans. As a result, it is possible that the U.S. consumers can be misled into believing that a particular cryptocurrency can limit supply of coins, while the company plans to add additional coins to the offer thereby reducing the value of the buyer's coins. If U.S. consumers without being deceived to purchase a particular cryptocurrency and information surrounding that cryptocurrency, it is not disclosed to the government, so consumers cannot afford their own protection government involvement in these programs.

If the US public wants government officials to do cryptocurrency manufacturers disclose information at the same level as companies trading publicly, of course it is likely that many of the current small cryptocurrencies will not be able to compete again offer some new options. After the Sarbanes-Oxley law was passed, small companies say earn less than one billion dollars and see their costs double. In addition, significant initial costs were required to maintain compliance department. As result, unless the cryptocurrency company has the necessary support margins the higher the cost, the less likely it is to stay in business. If disclosure was required for cryptocurrencies, more than less cryptocurrency development companies are out of business, possibly a the black cryptocurrency market can create those currencies that can or do not want to comply with the law. Historically, this has been seen many times. Harp writes that when the alcohol was banned during the ban, people turned to producing more dangerous alcohol as the light of the moon. When opioids are administered to require instructions for use, harmful compounds involving fentanyl began to be widely distributed.

Thus, history has set the example for the black market that poses a serious risk product. This problem is further exacerbated by the anonymity offered by digital cryptocurrency distribution. They may be the creators of cryptocurrency the desire to avoid control may turn to slightly safer transfer methods that go up risk of cryptocurrency theft.

Without control on the basis of protecting the financial security of consumers, the government may want to understand the use of cryptocurrency in illegal activities. Brown explained that the anonymous nature of cryptocurrency provides enough the possibility of criminals engaging in money laundering and illegal activities work with minimal risk of persecution. Although technology allows justice officials to be able to view blockchain, blockchain does not provide location information. I mean with the blockchain address information of the perpetrator, his or her actual location may not be known. This is because the perpetrator may be able to set up a virtual private network (VPN) that is able to hide his location. As it is not always possible to know location or identity of the criminal, tracking may almost certainly not be possible.

Additionally, according to Stokel-Walker, a new introduction cryptocurrency by Initial Coin Offerings (ICO) has created many new Ponzi schemes. These systems are aided by the lack of required disclosure and supervision by government also increases the risk of consumers losing money.

Lack of ICO rules makes fraudsters promise investors huge returns if they invest their money at a certain time, to travel with money and not bring it their promises. An article in the Money Life Journal (2018) highlights the latest example of this on BitConnect. The founders of BitConnect have offered cash payments to potential users BitConnect Coins. Payment from 40% monthly returns on investment. Unfortunately, the company did not meet their needs and those who bought the coins lost all that they had invested. Situations like these highlight potential dangers after being unchecked and unchecked crypto currency. Finally, Patil examined the frequency of robberies of sensitive information, a form of fraud used to gain personal information on the target. Patil explained, "In May 2013, it was founded that the source of the crime of identity theft that robbed a famous digital money company". These conditions can be completely avoided if government institutions control the industry, too only authorized exchange of selected cryptocurrency.

This way, users can access these exchanges without endangering their personal information. Ideally, it would be normal information that legal cryptocurrencies can only be accessed in this way, too criminal attempts to steal effective cryptocurrency sensitive information will end. Albuquerque and Callado concluded that it would take some form of government intervention to prevent it cryptocurrency fraud. However, the government should evaluate the potential benefits that the use of cryptocurrency brings to its users.

Finding Crypto-Market

After experiencing continued growth over the past few years, the cryptocurrencies market has been able to increase significantly in 2017, reaching more than 1,200%. Right now, there are a few hundred disbursements (with a total market value of more than EUR 300 billion), and above keep appearing regularly. To take full advantage of this emerging market and make a for a meaningful study, we have chosen to analyze the most well-known key features cryptocurrency Bitcoin and deal with the key features of the selected number of alternatives cryptocurrencies, better known as "Altcoins". Altcoins are different currencies than Bitcoin. In short, there are two types of Altcoins:

• Altcoins are built using the original Bitcoin open source protocol, with a number of changes its basic codes[116], to conceive a new coin with different characteristics.[117] Examples of such Altcoin is Litecoin.

• Altcoins are not based on the open source Bitcoin protocol, but have their own protocol and a distributed ledger. The best-known examples of such Altcoins are Ethereum and Ripple. This study will focus on the ten Altcoins that currently have the largest market capitalization. We have made this choice, not only on the basis of the current thunder of this are Altcoins within the "crypto-community", but also because they show a wide range of distinctions features. Some of them are based on the original Bitcoin open source protocol, while others build a completely new platform and / or eco-system. Some use the PoW method, others use another kind of compromise method. Most are considered anonymous, but some are said to be or anonymous (meaning the amount of coins their users own, send and receive is not visual, traceable or linked to the blockchain history (blockchain).

Bitcoin and beyond: 10 cryptocurrencies have a very high value market money

1. Bitcoin (BTC)

What is Bitcoin?

Bitcoin (BTC) is often described as a tangible, divisive currency (and at first glance) that is anonymous, which is not supported by the government or which is supported by any other legal entity, and which cannot be changed gold or any other commodity. At the heart of the creation of Bitcoin is the inscription "Bitcoin: a Peer-to-Peer Electronic Cash System" by Satoshi Nakamoto, published online in 2008. It was based on this text and idea transferred to it that the development of Bitcoin accelerated. Contribution to the mysterious nature of Bitcoin that so far it is not clear whether Satoshi Nakamoto is a real person, a pseudonym, or maybe even a gang of hijackers.

The visible Bitcoin coin suggests that Bitcoins generally do not take physical form. Therefore, a good representation of Bitcoin is probably a computer file stored on a personal computer or, via the Internet service, in a digital wallet. Just a visible bit of Bitcoins should, however, be they are not qualified. Respectfully, it is possible to print a combination of characters that make up Bitcoin and, later, to transfer such printing as a portable device. However, this should to be unusual, therefore, cannot be explained in detail here.

Bitcoin is based on the PoW consensus approach. The issue of Bitcoins occurs through a process called "mines" (see also above). Again, such a process is all its public elements available with open source software - including that people voluntarily make their own computers available on the Bitcoin network to solve complex mathematical problems.Computers that know to solve such problems (and, as a result, they are able to create so-called "blocks" of transactions rewarded with Bitcoins. The amount of Bitcoins that can be generated by mining is limited: the Bitcoin system is designed so that the development of blocks in time will be rewarded with a gradual decrease Bitcoins and that there will never be more than 21 million Bitcoins.

The fact that the creation and proliferation of Bitcoins is automatic and determined by the system itself means it exists there is no need for intermediate organization / authority to issue Bitcoins. The limited amount of Bitcoins, as well as the fact that Bitcoins conversion rates are such determines supply and demand, with the exception of a governmental body that is able to intervene (e.g. printing more money), resulting in higher Bitcoins price fluctuations.

b. Bitcoin operates on an open, unauthorized blockchain

Bitcoin blockchain is a typical example of an open, unlicensed blockchain. Anybody can join or leave the Bitcoin social network at your discretion, unless (before-) is authorized by any (intermediate) organization. All it takes to join the Bitcoin network and add transactions to the ledger is a computer where the appropriate software is installed.

c. Bitcoin is converted directly into fiat currency

Bitcoin can be purchased and converted directly into fiat currency in a wide range of crypto currency exchanges (e.g. Coinbase, Kraken, Anycoin Direct137, Lunco). In all currently used cryptocurrensets, Bitcoin is one of the easiest currency to convert to fiat money.

d. Bitcoin is a form of trading

Bitcoin (BTC) is recognized as the official source of revenue for the largest amount (online) vendors, among them various large companies (e.g. Microsoft, Expedia, Playboy, Virgin Galactic, LOT Polish Airlines). As a result it can be qualified as an exchange.

e. Bitcoin is an anonymous counterfeit currency

Bitcoin is often seen as an anonymous currency: although everyone can guarantee a series of transactions on the basis of public book, at first glance there is nothing in the system that links Bitcoins to individuals. However, this unknown character is far from perfect. Technically, although it is very complicated and expensive - to identify the parties after the Bitcoin transaction by delivery together the features associated with such work. In other words, Bitcoin is not something that is completely unknown money, but an unknown counterfeit coin.

Ethereum (ETH)

a. What is Ethereum?

Ethereum, launched in July, 2015, is a power-sharing platform using so-called "smart contracts". Smart contracts are "self-made contracts" or operating systems that work in a systematic way with the exception of any downtime (i.e., the blockchain has never been down, it always works), research, fraud or interference by a third party. Ethereum has far more potential than pure P2P digital currency like Bitcoin. In simple terms, it is like a smartphone operating system on top of software applications can be built. Speaking of technology, the Ethereum platform itself is not a cryptocurrency. However, like other open ones, with unlicensed blockchains, Ethereum requires a kind of on-chain value to encourage transactions network authentication (i.e. payment method for network nodes using jobs).

This is where the traditional Ethereum "ether" (ETH) cryptocurrency comes into operation. Ether not only allows smart contracts to be built on the Ethereum platform (i.e. it burns them), but and serves as an exchange (especially in the context of ITOs, as many tokens do purchased with ether). Like Bitcoin, Ethereum currently uses the PoW concordance method, but is slowly moving towards it adoption of the compliance method PoS, better known as Casper Protocol. The development of Ethereum is promoted and supported by the "Ethereum Foundation", a Swiss non-profit organization, founded by the founders of Ethereum. Bulk ether was "previously mined" (i.e. mine / created before the coin was officially introduced to the public) by its founders and sold crowd sale to pay for development costs and to fund Ethereum Foundation.

b. Ethereum uses an open, unlicensed blockchain

Like Bitcoin, Ethereum is a prime example of an open, unlicensed blockchain. Anyone may join or leave the Ethereum network at its own discretion, without prior authorization by any organization.

c. Ether (ETH) is converted directly into fiat currency

Ether (ETH) can be purchased and converted into fiat currency on various cryptocurrencies exchanges (e.g. Coinbase, Kraken).

d. Ether (ETH) is a form of exchange

Like Bitcoin, ether (ETH) is accepted as a payment method with a growing number of merchants (e.g. TapJets, Overstock). So it is also a way of trading.

e. Ether (ETH) is an anonymous counterfeit coin

Like Bitcoin, ether (ETH) can be classified as an anonymous or unknown counterfeit coin.

3. **Ripple (XRP)**

a. What is Ripple?

Ripple is an open source, P2P-enabled digital payment platform that allows for fast money transfers regardless of type (e.g. US Dollar, Yen, Bitcoin) was launched in 2012 by the independent company Ripple (Labs), Inc. Ripple (Labs), Inc, in charge of continuous development of Ripple protocol, the first company to acquire "BitLicense" on a case of institutional use of digital assets from the New York Department of Financial Services and gaining the support of many major players in the financial services industry, such as Bank La America Merill Lynch, Santander, etc. Following the launch of Ripple, the founders of Ripple launched the cryptocurrency XRP. XRP built to be bridge money to allow financial institutions to pay cross-border payments very quickly and cheaper than they can do with using worldwide payment networks available today, which is possible it is slow and involves many intermediaries (i.e. banks). However, in practice, the Ripple payment platform does not need bridge funding to really work. According to Ripple, XRP can handle more than 1,500 transactions per second. Although it was originally developed and intended for business use, currently adopted a large number of cryptocurrency users. Ripple (XRP) is not based on PoW or PoS authentication method transaction, but uses its own specific compliance protocol. The full XRP offer "fully pre-dug" (or better: created at the beginning of the coin) founders. Currently, held as follows:

- 8,102,265,714 XRP hosted by Ripple (Labs), Inc.

- 39,189,968,239 XRP distributed171; and

- 52,700,000,024 XRP is included in the escrow to ensure XRP provision at any time Time. Unlike the founders of Ethereum, Ripple developers did not sell part of the XRP with crowdsale over. XRP Creation to Support Ripple (Labs), Inc. The company was privately funded. At present, it is not entirely clear what XRP (primarily owned by Ripple (Labs), Inc.) is or will be it is still widely distributed in the future.

b. Ripple operates on a community-approved blockchain

Unlike Bitcoin and Ethereum, Ripple operates on an approved blockchain. This is because Ripple (Labs) Inc., a company behind Ripple (XRP), decides who can act as a proof of action its network. The blockchain itself is considered public, as it can be accessed and viewed by anyone.

c. Ripple (XRP) is converted directly into fiat currency

Like Bitcoin, XRP can be directly converted into fiat currency in various crytocurrency exchanges (e.g. Kraken, LiteBit175, Anycoin Direct, Bitsane).

d. Ripple (XRP) is an exchange method

Ripple (XRP) is accepted as a payment method with a growing number of (online) merchants various goods and services (e.g. e-cigarettes, honey, coffee). Recently there has been a buzz and online speculation that Amazon may be looking to use Ripple in the near future.

e. Ripple (XRP) is a counterfeit coin

Like Bitcoin, Ripple (XRP) can qualify as an anonymous counterfeit coin.

4. Bitcoin Cash (BCH)

a. What is Bitcoin Cash?

Bitcoin Cash (BCH) is a P2P digital currency created on August 1, 2017 and based on the original Bitcoin algorithm SHA-256 PoW, however there are some changes to its basic code. Bitcoin Cash is what is known in the crypto community as a "strong fork" of the Bitcoin blockchain. It is the result of two very different ideas about the future of Bitcoin and the Bitcoin blockchain, where Bitcoin blockchain is divided into two possible alternatives. In short, some Bitcoin developers wanted to increase the block size limit from 1MB to 8MB, reduce transaction costs and improve confirmation times, while others have different plans. Because the public could not reach a consistently, a new cryptocurrency Bitcoin Cash was created. Like Bitcoin, Bitcoin Cash uses the PoW method, which means it can be mined. This especially about Bitcoin Cash However, and the direct result of the hard fork, is that anyone holding Bitcoin when Bitcoin Cash was created (i.e. 1st August 2017 - 13:16 UTC) also became owns the same amount of Bitcoin Cash. Any Bitcoin acquired after that period follows the original method also does not include Bitcoin Cash.

b. Bitcoin Cash operates on an open, unauthorized blockchain

In fact, a "strong fork" does not change a blockchain type of currency. In other words, Bitcoin money also operates on an unauthorized open blockchain, such as Bitcoin.

c. Bitcoin Cash is converted directly into fiat currency

Like Bitcoin, Bitcoin Cash can be easily converted into fiat currency and vice versa by number cryptocurrency trading (e.g. Coinbase, Kraken, LiteBit).

d. Bitcoin Cash is an exchange method

Bitcoin Cash can be used to pay for a growing network of goods and services (eg jewelry, food, games, and telecom) in many online marketplaces and forums (e.g. OpenBazaar,

Bitcoin Cash initiative). As a result, Bitcoin Cash may be eligible as an exchange.

e. Bitcoin Cash is an anonymous counterfeit currency

Although Bitcoin Cash is a strong fork of Bitcoin, it does not differ much from its original form. Icon as well as an unknown counterfeit coin.

5. Litecoin (LTC)

a. What is Litecoin?

Like Bitcoin, Litecoin (LTC) is an open source cryptocurrency for P2P. Founded in

October 2011 and is based on the so-called Scrypt PoW algorithm, which uses the original Bitcoin algorithm SHA-256 PoW.195 Litecoin is often described as 'silver' in Bitcoin gold. Apart from the fact that it uses a different algorithm, it differs from Bitcoin in two ways. First, and this results in the use of the Scrypt PoW algorithm, Litecoin offers very fast transaction speed than Bitcoin. The time required to produce a block in Bitcoin BC is about ten 1977 minutes, while the average block creation time on the Litecoin blockchain is almost 2.5 minutes.

Second, the total offer for Litecoin has 84 million coins, which is much higher than 21 million Bitcoin offer limit.

b. Litecoin works on an open, unlicensed blockchain

Like Bitcoin, Litecoin runs on an open, unauthorized blockchain. All it takes to join network download software for open source software.

c. Litecoin is converted directly into fiat currency

Litecoin can be purchased with fiat currency at a cryptocurrency exchange rate (e.g. BTCDirect200, LiteBit, Coinbase, Anycoin Direct) and can, on that exchange, easily exchanged for fiat money.

d. Litecoin is a form of exchange

Litecoin is accepted as a payment method with a growing number of online retailers. Like Bitcoin, it also builds a trading platform.

e. Litecoin is an anonymous counterfeit coin

Like Bitcoin, Litecoin is an anonymous counterfeit currency. Everyone can confirm the LTC series transactions on the basis of a public record, which will make it technically possible to identify coins and / or receiver.

f. Litecoin and "Atomic Swaps" case

It should be noted that the Litecoin community has recently introduced new technologies to a crypto-world called "atomic swap". Simply put, atomic exchange makes P2P cross-chain exchange or trading of one cryptocurrency to another cryptocurrency, without necessity of a third person. For example, if Anna had one Bitcoin and wanted 100 Litecoins in return, she could do it you usually have to go through a trade (i.e. a third party) and pay a certain amount to get this trade done.

Suppose Jeff owns 100 Litecoins and instead wants one Bitcoin, and then has an atom in exchange Anna and Jeff were able to trade their Coins on their own. Now, in making an atom the exchange is not so simple. First of all, as it is still a common thread, the introduction of atomic exchange technology requires a lot of IT knowledge. For example, a link should be made between two cryptocurrencies blockchains, which require the implementation of an IT-protocol known as the crypto-community "Lightning Protocol". In addition, both blockchains must share the same cryptographic function (e.g. SHA-256 function) for atomic fluctuations.

While we they are not yet about to trade cross-chain friendly user, the emergence of atomic exchanges technology presents a new set of challenges.

6. Stellar (XLM)

a. What is Stellar?

Like Ripple, Stellar is an open source, distributed payment infrastructure. Stellar was created in 2014 by one of the founders of Ripple. Its goal is to connect people with affordable financial services to fighting poverty and developing individual strengths. Stellar can also be used to build smart contracts it is not based on the PoW or PoS compliance process, but has its own specific compliance protocol. Stellar is home to the cryptocurrency Lumen (XLM). In short, lumens are used to pay for transactions in the Stellar network; they contribute to the global financial system as well make transactions between different currencies quickly and securely.

The Stellar development is sponsored by the non-profit organization Stellar.org (compiled in 2014 as a nonprofit company in the U.S. State of Delaware), offering the development of tools and good community programs around the Stellar network and investment. Its employees enter the code into the network, but the network itself is completely called outside the organization. Similar to the cryptocurrency Ripple XRP, the total number of Stellar Lumens is "pre-dug". Managed by Stellar.org is tasked with distributing free Lumens, as follows:

- 50% will be given to individuals (through direct registration process);

- 25% will be given to partners (through a specific partnership program);

- 20% given to Bitcoin and XRP owners; and

- 5% is set for operating costs of Stellar.org.

The actual distribution is not done simultaneously, but over time in the number of cycles.

b. Stellar is running on an unauthorized blockchain

Unlike Ripple, Stellar runs on an unauthorized blockchain. Anyone can join the network at will, and, if certain conditions are met, confirm the transaction without prior authorization or testing by anyone general manager.

c. Lumens (XLM) are converted directly into fiat currency

Lumens (XLM) can be converted directly into fiat currency by cryptocurrency trading as

LiteBit (up to a maximum of EUR 500 (per purchase)) or Kraken.

d. Lumens (XLM) is NOT a real exchange method yet

Currently, therefore, it seems that Lumens (XLM) can only be used to pay for Stellar promotional stickers breakfast at the local bar in Arkansas216 and sprouts217. Although this proves that they are gradually being adopted as a payment method, they are not the true method of trading yet, at least when you compare it with the coins mentioned above.

e. Lumens (XLM) are anonymous counterfeit coins

All transactions on the Stellar network are public, but cannot be easily linked to their users. As a result, Stellar Lumens (XLM) may qualify as anonymous counterfeit coins.

7. Cardano (ADA)

a. What is Cardano?

Like Ethereum, Cardano is designed and continuously developed as a speaker over what is intelligent international contracts and applications (called "Dapps") can be processed. Cardano Project started in 2015220, and was officially released to the public in September 2017221. Based on that known as the Ouroboros PoS algorithm.

Cardano Forum is home to an open source cryptocurrency (ADA) . Ada can be used to send and receive digital currencies. It burns the Cardano platform, like a kind of money "Ether" is heating up the Ethereum platform. In short, Cardano aims to improve rating, security, governance, and collaboration with it traditional financial systems and regulations, by learning and improving the lessons learned Bitcoin and Ethereum communities. What separates Cardano from Ethereum, and many other cryptocurrensets, is that it is (one first) blockchain projects will be developed and designed from a scientific philosophy by the team leading scholars and engineers. Another significant difference is that, at present, cryptocurrency Ada (ADA) can only be stored in Cardano Daedalus' digital wallet.

The Cardano project currently has three major participants that each has a different role:

• The Swiss-based Cardano Foundation, which aims to standardize, protect and promote

• Cardano technology and eco-system;

• IOHK, a blockchain engineering company responsible for building the Cardano blockchain; and

• Emurgo, a company responsible for promoting commercial applications built on Cardano ecosystem.

Similar to Ethereum (cf. ether), a good number of Ada was "previously mined" (i.e. mine / previously created) coin introduced to the public) by its founders and sold in a crowded area to pay for development costs.

b. Cardano uses unauthorized and licensed blockchains

Cardano's Ouroboros PoS algorithm allows the platform to operate without a license and is licensed blockchains.

c. Ada (ADA) is converted directly into fiat currency

The Ada fee (ADA) can be converted directly into fiat currency. However, we found that, at currently, only one cryptocurrency exchange offers the option to directly convert Ada (ADA) into Euro, is

LiteBit and only comes with a maximum value of EUR 500 (per purchase). Ada, on the other hand, can be easily replaced by other cryptocurrencies (for example by using exchanges like Bittrex or Binance). These cryptocurrencies can be converted into fiat money.

d. Ada (ADA) is NOT a real way to trade right now

Our research shows that, at present, Ada can only be used to pay for a limited number of services (e.g. Hotel Ginebra Barcelona accepts payment by Ada). While this proves that Ada is gradually being accepted as a payment method, it is not a real trading method yet, at least not if compare the coins mentioned above. However this can change quickly.

e. Ada (ADA) is an anonymous counterfeit coin

Like the cryptocurrencies analyzed above, Ada can qualify as an anonymous counterfeit currency. It is interesting to note however - and to our knowledge, incomparable - that we know customer standards (KYC) used during the first Ada donation.

8. IOTA (MIOTA)

a. What is IOTA?

IOTA, launched in 2016234, is an open source ecosystem that people and equipment can transmit value (i.e. money) and / or data without any service charges in an unreliable, unauthorized, and a divided environment. In short, IOTA uses certain technologies that are said to be much larger than technology behind many other coins, and it promises a faster transaction speed. Like cryptocurrencies analyzed above, IOTA is based on distributed ledger technology. However, unlike the others cryptocurrencies, the widespread IOTA ledger do not cover transactions collected (transaction) "blocks" and is stored in consecutive chains (i.e. not "blockchain"), but in the stream each transaction is tied together. IOTA is based on what is known as directed acyclic graph (DAG) . Because the action is intertwined, this technology is also targeted as "Tangle".

Instead of requiring miners to do a PoW calculation and verify internal trading blocks in exchange for "mineral" coins, IOTA network participants made the agreement themselves confirming the two previous actions each time they wish to do a new job. Currently, IOTA is still very young. This is seen, among other things, as in order to the network is fully secure and all transactions must be digitally signed in a special network area (i.e. "Coordinator"). Because this affects the real network status of the division, the development of IOTA the team is working hard on the review to remove this special node by the end of 2018. The IOTA eco-system is being developed, supported, developed and maintained by "IOTA Foundation ", a German nonprofit foundation, founded by the founders of IOTA. IOTA created and released the so-called "founder addresses". Most sold IOTA founders to the crowd to cover development costs and to support IOTA Foundation.

b. IOTA uses an unrestricted distributed ledger

IOTA is not based on blockchain technology, but incorporates different uses for distribution ledger technology. It is - to put it in the words of its developers - it is intended to be (coming) public and an unauthorized spinal internet protocol for objects that enable real interaction between all devices.

c. IOTA is directly converted into fiat currency

The IOTA cryptocurrency (MIOTA) can be converted directly into fiat currency (like the Euro). However, our research shows that, at the moment, only one cryptocurrency exchange offers the option directly convert IOTA (MIOTA) to Euro, to CoinFalcon IOTA, on the other hand, can be easily replaced by other cryptocurrencies (for example by using exchanges similar to Binance). These cryptocurrencies can be converted into fiat currency.

d. IOTA is NOT an exchange method

It seems that at present there are no (online) vendors who accept IOTA as a payment method certain goods or services. IOTA is therefore not a trade-off. It will not be released yet, to be one in the future (imminent).

e. IOTA is an anonymous counterfeit coin

Apart from IOTA's unique eco-system, like other cryptocurrencies it is transparent and public letter available, meaning that one of the IOTA users sees the IOTA balance of that user and IOTA components transaction history. Like Bitcoin, IOTA can thus qualify as an anonymous counterfeit currency.

9. NEO (NEO)

a. What is NEO?

Like Ethereum and Cardano, NEO is an open source blockchain platform over its smartest international contracts and applications (called "Dapps") can be processed. NEO, sometimes referred to like "Chinese Ethereum", was originally introduced under the name "Antshares" in February, 2014. The project was renamed "NEO" in June 2017. In short, the NEO project aims to digitize assets and automate digital management property, in order to form the so-called "smart economy" (i.e. an economy in which parties can agree agreement without the need for trust). Like Ethereum (cf. "ether"), NEO itself is technically not a cryptocurrency. Traditional NEO currenc called "GAS". In simple terms, GAS is the amount that must be paid to be allowed to use the NEO network. One it can actually mean that the stadium is on fire. What's something about the NEO platform (once splits with Ethereum and Cardano plaforms) to hold digital "NEO" value (which can best be described as a kind of crypto-asset hybrid) automatically generates the amount of GAS over time. NEO is based on a consensus approach known to the crypto-like Byzantine mission community Fault Tolerance (dBFT) algorithm, which can support 10,000 transactions per second. The full provision of NEO "was previously mined"; part of it was sold at a public auction and partly headed by the NEO Council (i.e. the project founders' team) to support development as well maintenance of the NEO ecosystem.

b. NEO operates on an approved blockchain

To become a verifier of the transaction (i.e. node) on the NEO network, the verification candidate to

(i) elect a NEO development team and (ii) vote for the NEO community (i.e. those hold NEO) . These features are common in blockchain enabled.

c. NEO is converted directly into fiat currency, GAS does not exist

NEO can be directly converted into fiat currency. However, our research shows that, at the moment, only one cryptocurrency exchange offers the option to directly convert NEO into Euro, to Anycoin Direct. NEO GAS native currency currently cannot be converted directly to fiat currency. Both NEO and GAS, however, can be easily exchanged with other cryptocurrencies (e.g. through exchanges similar to Bittrex). These cryptocurrencies can be converted into fiat money.

d. NEO's GAS IS NOT an exchange method

While NEO works closely with major technology companies such as Microsoft, its native currency is GAS it is not an exchange method (nor is it NEO itself). Contrary to the number of other currencies mentioned above, our research did not reveal any online merchants willing to accept NEO coins as a means payment. Some argue that GAS is not actually intended to be a real means of trade. However, the same was said of Ethereum currency ether (ETH). With that in mind, it would not be so it is completely out of the question that GAS (or NEO itself) may be the future exchange system.

e. NEO's GAS is an anonymous counterfeit coin

In fact, GAS NEO may be eligible as an anonymous or anonymous counterfeit coin, such as a coin analyzed above. However, the main developers of NEO are currently actively working on the concept that will allow smart contract codes to bind what is called "digital ownership" in the real world ownership. It is quite impossible - yet it is not yet clear - that this technology will also affect the anonymous fake character of GAS.

10. Monero (XMR)

a. What is Monero?

Monero (XMR) is an open source cryptocurrency for P2P "focused on autonomy and resistance to research transactions". Founded in April 2014265 and based on CryptoNote POW algorithm. Monero is specially designed to allow its users to perform tasks anonymously. It is said to be automatically encrypted. In particular, it uses cryptography to protect both sending and receiving addresses (i.e. 'keys'), and transaction costs. Monero (XMR) seems to be a complete failure.

This means that two XMR units can always they can be exchanged jointly and there will be no blocking of certain XMR units by vendors either exchanges due to their association in previous works. Unreasonable cryptocurrencies, like him Bitcoin and Litecoin, in theory, are at risk of being banned from the list; if used illegally purpose in the past, then such history will be contained in the blockchain forever unlike other Coins, Monero (XMR) has not been mined before.

b. Monero operates on an unauthorized blockchain

Like Bitcoin, Monero (XMR) uses an unauthorized blockchain. Anyone can join the network. Voluntarily, unless otherwise authorized or inspected by any central administrator.c. Monero is directly converted into fiat currency Monero (XMR) can be converted directly to fiat currency in digital currency trading. (E.g. LiteBit, Anycoin Direct, Kraken).

d. Monero is a form of exchange

Monero is accepted as a payment method with a growing number of online retailers. Like Bitcoin, it also builds a trading platform.

e. Monero is an unknown coin

In a fully fledged blockchain, such as Bitcoin or the Ethereum blockchain, transactions are permanent it is clearly guaranteed and traceable by anyone. Actually - though this may not be an easy task – posting and receiving addresses of such activities can be linked to the true identity of life. That's where Monero encourages it to be different. It sets itself up as a safe, confidential and inaccessible place crypto currency. This high level of anonymity is achieved using two different strategies:

- Ring Confidential Activities ("RingCT"); and

- Private addresses.

i. Ring Confidential Actions

First, Monero uses what is called the Ring Confidential Transactions. RingCT covers the process of the signature ring and what it refers to in the crypto-community as a private transaction concept:

- Ring signatures include or 'associate' user account keys and public keys received from them Monero blockchain to create, what can be called a 'ring' for potential signers, which means

External viewers cannot link a signature to a specific user. Included for theft addresses (see below) allow for complete anonymity of both senders and recipients for XMR;

- Confidential activity adds another layer of privacy to 'compile' with encryption the value of each price. In addition to producing real numbers, they include cryptographic evidence that the total input value is the same as the output value.

ii. Privacy Addresses

Second, and in addition to RingCT, Monero also uses secret addresses. Private addresses generated randomly, one-time addresses created for each transaction by the sender on behalf of the recipient. All payments sent to the recipient are forwarded to these addresses, to ensure that there are no links in the blockchain between the sender and recipient address. In other words, private addresses block communication on the blockchain. However, without using RingCT, the original sender of coins will now be able to track the coins if they are not removed by the recipient by pointing to the results in the blockchain. RingCT mask these effects, make it what is being done is completely unattainable.

iii. Kovri project

It should be noted that the community of (important) developers and specialists of cryptography in the background Monero is currently working on a project to add another layer of privacy to the Monero ecosystem by roaming and encrypting XMR sales via I2P Invisible Internet Project nodes. Usage I2P will block the vendor IP address and provide additional security to the network caution. This project, in which the alpha version is currently available, is better known to cryptocommunity as the Kovri project.

11. Dash (DASH)

a. What is Dash?

Dash (DASH), formerly known as Darkcoin280, is an open source cryptocurrency P2P based on secrecy. It was first launched in January 2014 and is based on what is known as the X11 PoW algorithm exactly Dash, and what makes it different from most other currencies, is that it has a two-phase network. The Dash blockchain is protected by so-called "masternodes" over PoW by miners. In short, a masternode is a server connected to a Dash network that verifies something minimum level of performance and performance to perform certain functions related to PrivateSend as well InstantSend (Dash anonymity and instant messaging features).

Trading a normal cryptocurrency currency can be very time consuming (i.e. it can take a while anywhere between a few minutes and over an hour). This is because the blocks are enough it should pass to ensure that what is being done is irreversible and at the same time not an attempt double the amount already spent. Dash deals with this issue using its own masternode. network. Masternodes can be called to build voting queues to check that a the submission is valid and if so, the 'masternodes' key' input once spread this information on the network, successfully promising that the work will be included blocks are then mined and do not allow any other amount for these entries during verification time ". As a result Dash is said to be able to compete with almost instantaneous transactions programs, such as credit cards.

b. Dash runs on an open, unauthorized blockchain

Like Monero, Dash operates on an unauthorized blockchain. Anyone can join the network at will, unless otherwise authorized or inspected by any senior director.

c. Dash is converted directly into fiat currency

Dash (DASH) can be converted directly into fiat currency by various cryptocurrency transactions (e.g. Anycoin Direct, Kraken).

d. Dash is an exchange method

Like Monero, Dash is accepted as a payment method with a slightly growing price in the internet marketers. As a result Dash has also developed a trading platform.

e. Dash is an anonymous (optional) coin

Like the Bitcoin blockchain, the Dash blockchain appears automatically, which means more often speech is always clearly confirmed and tracked on the blockchain. Providing its users for real financial privacy, Dash offers the option to use a feature called PrivateSend. PrivatePost is obscure the source of user revenue through a process known as "mixing".

Similar regulatory challenges in the fight against money laundering, terrorist financing and tax evasion via cryptocurrencies

1. Anonymity

An important issue that needs to be addressed in order to adequately holds cryptocurrencies once cryptocurrency players, especially users, illegally disclose anonymity complete anonymity of anonymity- fake, around them. This is a very big problem anti-money laundering and anti-terrorism support: anonymity prevents cryptocurrency transactions from adequate recruitment, allowing for shady transactions to take place without a regulatory perimeter, which allows criminal organizations to use cryptocurrencies to obtain easy access to "clean money" (both income / expenditure). It has to do with terrorist finances, the story of Ali Shukri Amin who gave instructions via Twitter on how to use Bitcoin to conceal a financial offer Daesh is a wonderful example of the dangers posed by the anonymity surrounding crypto currency. Anonymity is also a major problem when it comes to tax evasion. Entry into a fruitful cryptocurrency what you do without paying taxes is tax evasion. But, when the tax officer does not know who is entering taxed transactions, due to the anonymity involved, are unable to identify or authorize this tax to flee. This makes cryptocurrencies an attractive option for tax evaders. Individual analysts' tools like Bitcoin have even been described as "future tax havens". That being said, and as seen in our review of cryptocurrencies above, it should be noted that some cryptocurrencies are anonymous, which means that when a great effort is made as well as the sophisticated techniques used, it is possible for the authorities to obtain the ownership of the users. While this may already be helpful in combating money laundering, terrorist financing and taxation avoidance of other cases, does not allow a standard way to deal with money laundering, terrorist support and tax evasion in general: finding out who this way is is also very complicated it is too expensive to be a standard response to this issue - and moreover, it will not lead to that any result. New initiatives such as the Investigation of Sub-Market Markets ("TITANIUM") project, may change this at some point, but it is too early to say how much in any case, a structured control system is desirable.

2. A cross-border nature

In addition to the anonymity, the environment that crosses the border of cryptocurrencies, crypto markets and crypto players are a big challenge for regulators. One of the problems e.g. that crypto markets also crypto players can be found in areas that do not have active cash transfers as well terrorist financial controls exist. Environment that crosses the boundaries of crypto currencies, crypto markets and crypto players probably mean that the rules will only suffice if taken from the international level enough.

2. There is usually no mediator

Another important factor that challenges the fight against money laundering, terrorist financing and tax evasion that there is usually no intermediary mediator, such as the issuer, who usually is focus area of control. Therefore, an important question is which players in the crypto market regulation should be instituted, in the absence of a mediator.

3. Cryptocurrencies fall between the cracks

The current European legal framework fails to address the issues raised above. Bangu simply no laws exposing the anonymity associated with crypto-currencies, which raises a question whether they are taken at the right level or by those who use the supernatural. Due to the lack of laws exposing anonymity, strict laws are not yet known you already have cryptocurrencies in an area that you do not completely miss. This is especially true in law a tax exchange framework.

The framework will not be activated: to exchange information, authorities must have it in the first place. For the same reasons, the current EU framework for tax evasion, which is linked to, among other things, tax exemptions in the context of goods corporate transfers, however, do not work well when it comes to crypto currencies, due to their anonymity and an easy-to-hide environment. In order to be taxable, tax authorities must know the basics of taxation and when it comes to cryptocurrencies this is very difficult. Another example is related to freezing and seizure. Obviously, it is disputed that crypto currency is already at the level of relevant European laws.

Property within these rules refers to the structure of any meaning, whether physical or non-physical, movable or immovable, and legal documents or tools that prove the theme or interest in the area. Well, that's acceptable cryptocurrencies are within the definition of this definition: they can be seen as intangible assets property. However, to leave a few examples of success stories aside, the rules do not work well. Reason and, the same: in order to stop and seize crypto currency you need to know that the criminal has them, and this is what is being blocked by anonymity surrounding them with secret money. Therefore, the essence of the matter is how we can reveal the anonymity associated with cryptocurrency trading so that you can track illegal transactions.

5. Tough separation line with cybersecurity, data protection and privacy

Admittedly, encryption, which is basically what happens in the context of cryptocurrencies, is the case an effective way for citizens and businesses to protect themselves from IT abuse technologies, such as hacking, identity theft and personal data, fraud and disclosure confidential information. However, encryption can also be used by criminals, e.g. use of cryptocurrencies for money laundering or terrorist financing, making it difficult to enforce the law criminal investigation of authorities. Therefore, a thin line between the storage of the solid encryption to protect cybersecurity, data protection and privacy on the other hand, while providing opportunities for law enforcement to access information for criminal purposes and investigation with appropriate protections on the other hand, as noted by Europeans Commission. We raise this issue, but we will not discuss online security, data protection as well privacy issues in this study. That would be beyond scope.

6. Do not throw the baby in the bath water: technology

Cryptocurrencies use smart technology. From a law enforcement perspective, to present crypto player accountability systems should prevent this technology from being used especially for bad intentions, but at the same time do not prevent new technologies from what happened. Therefore, legal action must always be balanced in order to address the problem illegal conduct while at the same time not being choked by technological innovations at birth. This is a feature of the specific relevance of this study. Cryptocurrencies operate on a blockchain or other technology. This technology is completely legal and offers many benefits of innovation many legal entities, including businesses and the public sector. For example it has been suggested that blockchain technology could be an effective defense against digital ransomware.

The idea is that with blockchain technology sensitive information can be stored in a a method of separation instead of placing in one place (as it is now). Storing information in an expanded location method makes it difficult to link information to a related person. Then again it is difficult know who to talk to for the ransom. In addition, there will be more copies of the information, to be made it is very difficult for criminals to catch them all to save them. Another barrier could be that attacking the information classification system will be easily visible to its participants. Other an example of a legal case for the use of blockchain technology for maximum profit can be obtained China, where the blockchain is used to combat tax fraud in the context of a partnership Tencent and Shenzhen national tax office.

When crypto money is used for criminal purposes, it is not the technology that should be the case targeted. On the contrary, illegal use should be directed. In particular, however, I exceptions can be made in well-defined situations, such as the mixing process used in the context of Dash and Monero's RingCT, secret addresses and Kovri project. This approach was adopted by the European Commission in developing its proposed amendment AMLD4315, as will be discussed later. In that regard, the Commission emphasized that the proposed measures have no adverse effects on the benefits and advances in technology presented with distributed ledger technology that is the basis for real money, including new ways of saying governments to reduce fraud, corruption, errors and costs of paperwork, established procedures new, modern ways in which governments and citizens work together, about data sharing, transparency and reliability, and the provision of new information on establishing ownership and acquisition of assets and intellectual property.

7. Status changes: AMLD5

As we will analyze further in this study, the European wave is changing. At the time of writing this explore new European laws on money laundering and terrorist financing in the last phase of adoption. These rules include measures to withdraw crypto money and (some) crypto players abroad of control darkness. Therefore, the regulatory approach adopted by the EU is to deal with cryptocurrencies and crypto players with money laundering laws and terrorist financing. As a last resort in the introduction, from a psychological point of view, the EU could have done this through other types of legislation, such as financial services law. That too would be a drag cryptocurrencies and crypto players have come out of the dark into light, even more so, e.g. proper crypto players would need a license.

As we will see further, this option, from insurance opinion, is not selected in this category. Following this we will discuss a new European framework for crypto and crypto currencies players in a position to combat money laundering and terrorist financing. We will start analysis by highlighting the background of the legal framework. After that, we'll be brief discuss the current framework. Later, a legal road to the next draft the forthcoming draft itself will be considered. Finally, two additions to the framework of will be briefly touched on, Transfers of Money Legislation and Financial Regulation Act, to ensure that cryptocurrencies exist in this regard regulations.

Money laundering and terrorist financing

1. In the background

The fight against money laundering and terrorist financing is a major issue worldwide society, including the EU. It has long been known that money laundering activities usually done internationally and therefore national measures are not sufficient. Recommendations for Financial Action Task Force ("FATF") - developed in 1990 and reviewed since from time to time - they are the backbone of an international anti-money laundering framework and terrorist financing. They are licensed in more than 180 countries, and they exist worldwide recognized as setting international standards. The European Union adopted its first Anti-Money Laundering Directive on 10 June 1991 ("AMLD1"). A framework to combat money laundering at the European Union level was needed for co-ordination measures in all Member States and to protect the stability of the financial system as a perfect. This First Anti-Money Laundering Order was later amended by the second Anti-Money Laundering Directive ("AMLD2"), before it was abolished and replaced by a third Anti-money. Laundering Directive ("AMLD3") the latter introduces anti-terrorism funding and including the revised FATF recommendations of 2003.

In February 2012, the FATF published a revised version its set of Recommendations. In line, the Commission reviewed the Third Amount of Money Laundering Order, which needed to be reviewed and complied with the 2012 FATF. Recommendations May 20, 2015 Revised anti-money laundering and anti-terrorism program a financial framework was adopted that significantly changed the existing EU legal framework designed to protect the financial system against money laundering and terrorist financing. The revised regulations contain the fourth Anti-Money Laundering Directive ("AMLD4") and EU Funds.

Transfer Regulation ("FTR") and provide a highly targeted and risk-oriented approach. AMLD4 aims to strengthen existing laws and make effective anti-money laundering and terrorist financing effective. AMLD4 was to be converted to Member States on the 26th the latest June 2017. From that day on, FTR also came into operation.

2. AMLD4

The main goal of AMLD4 is to prevent money laundering and terrorist financing. What is money laundering? Technically, the following behavior is money laundering, if you are committed deliberately:

a) The conversion or transfer of property, knowing that the property has been seized from a criminal a work or act of participating in that work, for the purpose of concealment or concealment illegal source of structure or assistance to any person involved in the commission such an act to avoid the legal consequences of that person's action;

b) To conceal or conceal actual identity, source, location, status, movement, right about, or ownership of property, by knowing that the property was seized from a criminal a work or act of participating in that work;

c) The acquisition, management or use of an asset, knowing, at the time of acquisition, that property taken from a criminal act or from an act of participation in that activity;

d) Participation, organization commitment, striving for commitment and support, support, motivation and to advise on the performance of any of the actions referred to in points a, b and c. In simple terms money laundering can be described as a process criminal acts are "cleansed" and brought to the legal economy so that their illegal origins can be hidden. In the context of the definition of currency trading, "asset" means assets of any kind, whatever tangible or intangible objects, moving or immovable, tangible or intangible, and legal documents or tools of any kind including electronic or digital, proof subject or interest in that property.

Money laundering will also be considered where jobs have created space to be washed and made in place of a third world. What is terrorist financing? This is defined as the provision or collection of funds, in any form, directly or indirectly, for the purpose of their use or for the information that they are supposed to be used, in whole or in part, to commit any offenses according to the definition of Sections 1 to 4 Council Decision 2002/475 / JHA Resolution on Terrorism. These are the cases in question deliberate actions that undermine their nature or essence can seriously damage a country or a country an international organization in which it has committed itself to the purpose of intimidating the people, or forcing a government or international organization to do or refrain from doing so to commit any act, which is acts that infringe upon or undermines the political, constitutional, national or international economic or social structures. They are considered terrorists charges: assault on a person's health that could result in death, assault on physical integrity a person, kidnapping or kidnapping, resulting in the destruction of the state or society location, transport system, infrastructure area, including information system, fixed forum placed on a continental shelf, public place or private property that may endanger human life or the result of severe economic losses, etc.

The difference between terrorist financing and money laundering is that in the case of terrorists financially, financial origins can be legal. A place of finance, i.e. financial support terrorists, that makes the whole treaty illegal. Theft of money on the contrary is a definition based on other crimes that cause trafficking in question. There is no definition of "investment" included in AMLD4. Legal theory prefers that it should have the same meaning as "property" under AMLD4; especially considering that such an approach would be consistent with FATF recommendations.

Rationed personae AMLD4 operates in so-called compulsory organizations. Because these mandatory structures are the entry point for money laundering and the financial needs of terrorists, sometimes too called "gatekeepers". Compulsory companies include: credit bureaux, financial institutions, a well-defined nature list or legal persons involved in the performance of their professional duties (under which auditors, outsiders accountants, tax advisers, bookkeepers and other independent legal professionals), trust or company service providers, real estate agents, other real estate agents made or received in cash at a cost of EUR 10,000 or more with gambling service providers. In addition, Member States are required to increase AMLD4 levels in whole or in part in order to professions and categories of work, with the exception of the responsible businesses mentioned above, are engaging in activities that are likely to be used for money laundering purposes or terrorist support. This means ongoing monitoring by Member States regarding money laundering and the risk of financing terrorists in their area and taking action when exposed to danger. If a business is a responsible entity and thus falls within AMLD4, it is subject to variability requirements, ultimately aimed at tracking financial information and having a preventative impact money laundering and terrorist financing.

An important requirement is that mandatory organizations should treat customers diligently if to establish business relationships, in which you do an equal part-time job EUR 15.000 or more, where there are allegations of money laundering or terrorist financing, whether of any reduction, release or limitation, where there is doubt about the authenticity or adequacy Pre-obtained customer identification data, etc. Proper customer diligence measures include among other things to identify the customer and verify his or her identity, to identify the beneficial owners and to take reasonable steps to ensure the identity of these persons, by conducting continuous monitoring of business, business relationships and risk profile.

Another important requirement is that when compulsory organizations know, suspect or have a valid reason to suspect that money, no matter how much money is involved, is a criminal advantage work or related to terrorist financing, should inform competent financial intelligence a unit ("FIU"), which all Member States must establish in order to prevent, identify and effective fight money laundering and terrorist financing, and provide it with all the necessary information. Everything Suspicious activities, including attempted transactions, should be reported. The FIU itself analyzes suspicious transactions. It disseminates the results of its analysis to the competent authorities where there are reasons to suspect money laundering, cases related to the claim or terrorist support. Because money laundering and terrorist financing are not restricted by borders, it is clear that FIUs need to cooperate and share information on a large scale possible, regardless of their organizational status. If liable businesses fail their duties under AMLD4, they may be authorized. AMLD4 wants that any such punishment must be effective, fair and not permissible. Moreover, and more generally, competent authorities should have the appropriate sanction toolbox, on an ongoing basis defined under AMLD4, which enables them to authorize violations of national provisions Exchange stocks AMLD4.

An important innovation of AMLD4 is the so-called profitable register. This is related to compulsory suspension of the central register 455 which includes information on beneficia business ownership and other legal entities. When mandatory organizations take appropriate customer action measures, information on beneficial ownership should be provided to them. It should also be informative reached by competent authorities and FIUs. Other people besides the competent authorities and FIUs are able to demonstrate legitimate interest in money laundering, terrorist financing, and related offenses, such as corruption, tax fraud and fraud, will also be provided access to beneficial ownership information, in accordance with data protection laws.

AMLD4 contains a variety of services related to relationships with third-party third-party risk organizations. First, responsible businesses should apply the improved level of due diligence of the customer when dealing with the environment persons or legal entities established in the high risk three countries identified by the Commission. In addition, reliance on third parties is established above developed by the Egmont Group, i.e. illegal network of FIUs for international promotion cooperation.

3. Cryptocurrencies under AMLD4

Are transactions in cryptocurrencies included in the AMLD4 range? Although there is

Scholarly debate on this, it is fair to say that it is very difficult, if not impossible, to extend the scope of AMLD4 to date for inclusion in cryptocurrency transactions. An insurmountable obstacle to crypto currencies to be included in the AMLD4 network connection element "assets" or "funds". As mentioned above, assets - and, of course, assets -

are defined as assets of any kind, whether tangible or non-existent, movable or immovable, tangible or intangible, and legal documents or tools of any kind including electronic or digital, title proof or interest in such goods. Although not written about cryptocurrencies, initially, this definition wide enough to integrate with crypto currency, as it can be seen as immovable goods for purposes of AMLD4.

An insurmountable obstacle, however, is that of a list of responsible businesses. There are no players in a cryptocurrency system, regardless of which cryptocurrency is involved, directly or indirectly included in the list of responsible organizations, not even crypto transactions. Therefore, the AMLD4 framework not only will it be attached to the crypto system; it will completely free you from the scope of AMLD4. This also came to the attention of the European Commission in 2016, which initiated legal action to bring about real money exchange forums with fund providers under the scope of AMLD in the future. The coming years of this inclusion in the AMLD framework will be specified after this. It is not intended to discuss all the steps taken, but only to highlight important steps, finally with the intention of making a better understanding of where the last one is results and policy choices emerged.

4. Coming age for the inclusion of cryptocurrencies in AMLD5354

a. First words: Terminology

Before we delve deeper into the age of cryptocurrency investing in AMLD5, we note that many policy documents use the term "virtual currencies" instead of cryptocurrencies. What is important in this study is that cryptocurrencies are a subset of virtual currency, more especially that kind of tangible currency with dual connections to the real economy. Therefore, in all of this analysis of the regulatory framework we refer to tangible investments, this includes cryptocurrencies. In addition, if we look at the exact range of definitions included in various policy texts, there is a clear tendency to direct crypto currencies with these definitions and not or to a lesser extent only the other virtual currencies only have them a direct or indirect link in the real economy.

b. Vision for the 2014 EBA on real money

An important first step in integrating the cryptocurrency system into the AMLD framework is the vision of the European Banking Authority in

2014 on real money. In this report the EBA advocates a comprehensive regulatory approach regarding financial performance over time. Ideally this is done by designing a control system that is aligned with the lines of the following features: to create the governing body of the tangible financial system namely must be accountable to the regulator, the requirements of appropriate customer diligence, eligibility and eligibility standards persons performing certain functions on the governing body, alternatives or other important matters market participants, mandatory inclusion in the EU Member States, transparent price structure and requirements against market abuse, authorization and corporate governance requirements, financial requirements, proof of secure IT systems, payment guarantee and refund requirements, the separation of tangible financial systems into common payment systems and international controls approach.

As a quick response, the EBA recommends incorporating market participants directly interactions between common and virtual currencies, such as virtual currency trading, in the scope of AMLD is 'as a corporate business' and thus subject to anti-money laundering and anti-terrorism financial requirements. According to EBA, this immediate response will 'protect' the regulated financial services from virtual financial systems, and will reduce those risks arising from interaction between the material financial systems and regulated financial services. Some things are equal, this is fast. The response, according to the EBA, will allow virtual currency schemes to establish and develop externally of the financial services sector, which includes the development of solutions that will satisfy the controls long-term demands.

None of these options were ultimately reserved by the European legislature: no draft was prepared is made up of tangible currencies, and EBA proposals to expand the scope AMLD followed during a review - which was ongoing at the time - which led to AMLD4.

c. Council invites

The momentum changed after the terrorist attacks in France. At the meetings held in December 2015, the Council of Europe concluded that the issue of terrorism was urgent. Following this, Council on 12 February 2016 emphasized the importance of immediate benefits progress in legal activities identified by the Commission, including in the virtual sector funds. Therefore, request the Commission to submit the proposed amendments to AMLD4 and if necessary in the Revised Payment Services Order ("PSD2") and Financial Management Regulation.

d. More than 100 Commission Risk Assessment

On June 26, 2017, the European Commission released its report on risk assessment money laundering and terrorist financing that affects internal markets and is cross-border activities (also called "Advanced Risk Assessment"). In its report to the Commission identified potential funds as potentially at risk of money laundering and terrorist financing risk affecting the domestic market. In general, the Commission appropriately identifies the anonymity of financial transactions as a general risk in all sectors, including related anonymity tangible money. Their anonymity features put an internal limit on identification as well monitoring opportunities. The Commission goes so far as to recommend Member States to expand already list of compulsory organizations for the use of Article 4 of AMLD4 to be considered which includes at least some cash exchanges with fund providers across the AMLD4 range.

e. Commission Impact Assessment compliant with AMLD5 proposal

In formulating a legislative proposal to amend AMLD4, the Commission made the comprehensive impact assessment ("Impact Assessment"). Impact Assessment acknowledges it the problem is that suspicious transactions made with real money are not adequately monitored by the authorities, who can link identity and transaction, mainly because of the ambiguity surrounding tangible funds and because of tangible financial systems as well partners (users (traders, suppliers, customers), 'miners', currency exchange forums, wallet providers) uncontrolled.

Most interesting are the potential regulatory responses to address this issue. According to Impact Assessment, the following.

i. The first option: targeted users, including buyers and sellers who use real money as an investment product or as an exchange to buy / sell products or services. Impact Assessment identifies two ways to raise user anonymity. First by mandatory user registration (option A). The second one is softer and less visible ' anonymity of voluntary user registration (option B). This option will not end anonymity, however, will allow anti-money laundering authorities to quickly verify their identity registered users.

ii. The second option: direct the exchange for real money

Also, Impact Assessment suggests two ways to move forward. The first is to make an exchange obligations under AMLD4 (option C), which refer, among other things, to customers who have to pay diligence requirements. The second way forward is to bring about real money exchange platforms under the PSD2 range (option D). PSD2 is superior to AMLD4. More than anti-money financial and anti-terrorist financial requirements that are automatically set for reference to AMLD4, PSD2 and establishes licensing liability for regulated organizations, small fee requirements, protection requirements, and consumer protection laws. This way forward, therefore, it is an additional burden of trade.

iii. Option 3: delivery providers are targeted directors

For the first and second options, the Impact Assessment suggests two possible actions, namely similar to the methods suggested for commercial suppliers, therefore: respectively to subdivide them width of AMLD4 (option E) or less than PSD2 width (option F). Why target only providers' fund providers? The reason for the Impact Assessment is that software wallet providers only provide applications or applications running on user hardware for access public information from a distributed book and access to the network. So, they are just technology service provider.

Custodian bag providers on the contrary have authority over the user a public and private key, making it possible to move away from a common financial perspective institutions that hold bank or payment accounts. Therefore, they need more attention.

iv. Optional testing

After consultation with the relevant stakeholders, the Impact Assessment assesses the need for it gatekeepers in charge of user ID control if required. In that, the vast majority of countries are members of the popular option C rather than D, which is why they make real money business forums that are responsible under AMLD4 instead of incorporating them into the PSD2 range. The options considered by fund providers were clearly not in the debate area either participant, although some Member States have expressed a preference for inclusion these in the AMLD4 range, instead of the PSD2 range. Generally, any option includes PSD2 therefore it has not been adopted by most Member States. They believed that this would provide the greatest possible benefit legitimacy of tangible assets and encourages consumers to believe that tangible investments are safe and sound products, which are not, according to various warnings of financial managers everywhere the globe is out.

The financial industry itself seems to approve of the law for two reasons: it can give them more flexibility and can help differentiate between bona-fide users as well criminals. Options that include user registration are obviously properly evaluated participants (i.e. buyers / users, professionals), which leads to the optional optional registration.

f. AMLD5 Commission Recommendation

In its fifth revision of AMLD ("Commission Proposal"), launched on 5 July 2016, the commission eventually adopted a method of incorporating both virtual currency transactions (defined as "Providers are actively involved and active in the exchange services between real money and fiat funds ") and fund providers (defined as" fund providers who provide end-to-end services verification requirements diligence control when exchanging virtual currency with fiat currency types, eliminating the anonymity associated with it such exchanges with fund providers, and report suspicious transactions to a competent FIU. In addition, virtual currency exchanges and savings wallet providers will require authorization either registered; apparently the Commission leaves the option between license and registration open. For valid legal reasons, the Commission also proposes the definition of the term "virtual currency": "a digital representation of value that may be issued by a central bank or public authority, or unnecessarily connected fiat money, but accepted by natural or legal persons as a means of payment and can transferred, stored or electronically ".

With regard to user registration, the Commission does not take immediate action. Rather, it is a commitment including its in-country risk assessment, which must be paid by 26 June 2019, if applicable, appropriate proposals, including, where appropriate, with regard to tangible funds, the ability to set up and maintain a central website that registers user ID and wallet addresses accessible to FIUs, as well as disclosure forms used by users of tangible funds. This, however, does not mean that users remain completely absent from the Commission's proposal. In particular, users are indirectly directed at how they manage their tangible investments through a provider's savings accountant or enter into cash-generating transactions court. These users can no longer be anonymous, due to the diligence of the customer requirements placed on the caregiver's wallet and physical exchange platforms. All other users remain offline (yet).

g. Updated EBA view

Following the Commission's recommendation, EBA published a review of its 2014 vision for virtual funds. The EBA welcomes this proposal as an important step in reducing some of the finances the risks of crime resulting from the use of tangible money. The EBA also supports the Commission a method of excluding tangible cash sales in the PSD2 range at present, provided a short period in which the Commission was asked to develop its recommendations. Includes such operations within the scope of PSD2 require analysis of the legal and business model, EBA oil. In addition, the EBA appears to still prefer a different and structured control system, the features he proposed in his 2014 vision. To achieve that, the EBA invites the Commission to immediately begin the full analysis required in the assessment that, if any, the control system will be most suitable for trading in real money. h. ECB's 2016 Vision on the Commission's recommendation

In addition to the EBA, the ECB also, on 12 October 2016, issued a report on the Commission. In that report the ECB strongly supports including financial exchanges with wallet suppliers who are not on the list of compulsory companies, and who need to be licensed or registered. The ECB, however, also expressed some concern, when that, however, was the case appropriate to control tangible anti-money laundering and terrorist financing, Regulation should not seek to encourage the widespread use of tangible funds. In addition, the ECB did technical comments related to the definition of financial terms, later downloaded to relaxation text, discussed later.

i. Debate in Parliament: the Commission's proposal was carefully considered by members of the European Parliament between 2016 and 2017.

A comprehensive report was adopted proposing a number of amendments. Of particular interest are the recommendations made by the Legal Affairs Committee of 18 January 2017. The Committee proposes to increase the scope of AMLD significantly in terms of virtual funds, for the purpose of installing real money exchange forums, fund providers, issuers, directors, coordinators and distributors of tangible funds, and regulators and suppliers of online payment systems. This is very broad and has the potential to deliver all the cash-generating service providers under the AMLD range. This has been the subject of so much legal criticism scope includes only technical service providers, such as miners cryptocurrencies, or simple not real, because there is no central issuer - as is the case with most cryptocurrencies.

In addition, the Legal Affairs Committee is of the view that combating related risks anonymity, national FIUs should be able to associate virtual currency addresses with the ownership of owner of tangible funds. Extensions are not taken from the Accord Text, which is analyzed later.

j. Text of Consensus

On 13 December 2017, and following the technical work thereafter, a temporary agreement was reached between Parliament and the Council regarding AMLD5, which led to a final agreement. This was officially adopted by the European Parliament at a meeting on 19 April 2018.368 May 14. In 2018, the Council approved the position of the European Parliament at the first reading. AMLD5 will enter came into operation on the twentieth day following its publication in the

Official Journal of the European The Member States of the Union will be required to apply the rules, regulations and administrative provisions it is required to comply with AMLD5 by no later than 10 January 2020. Overall, the Accepted Draft Agreement is in line with the Commission's Recommendation. Anyway, there there is a difference.

First, the Compromise text uses a variety of terms to integrate virtual currency exchange services once wallet providers not kept on the list of compulsory companies (change compared to Commission the proposal is marked after: "providers have participated virtual exchange services funds as well as fiat currencies and custodian wallet providers.

Secondly, the Compromise Text uses a slightly different definition of virtual currencies. More in particular, it defines virtual currencies as "a digital representation of value that is not issued or guaranteed by a central bank or a public authority, is not necessarily attached to a legally established currency, and does not possess a legal status of currency or money, but is accepted by natural or legal persons, as a means of exchange, and which can be transferred, stored and traded electronically" (the changes compared to the Commission Proposal are marked hereinafter: "a digital representation of value that is not issued or guaranteed by a central bank or a public authority, is not necessarily attached to a legally established currency, and does not possess a legal status of currency or money, but is accepted by natural or legal persons, as a means of exchange, and which can be transferred, stored and traded electronically").

Thirdly, a definition of "custodian wallet provider" ("an entity that provides services to safeguard private cryptographic keys on behalf of their customers, to hold, store and transfer virtual currencies") is included. Such a definition was not included in the Commission Proposal.

Fourthly, the Compromise Text is more precise on whether exchange platforms and custodian wallet providers should be licensed or registered: they should be registered (the changes compared to the Commission Proposal are marked hereinafter: "ensure that providers of exchange services between virtual currencies and fiat currencies, and custodian wallet providers, are registered").

The obligation for the Commission to assess the desirability of a (voluntary) registration of users in the course of its next supranational risk assessment, due by 26 June 2019, is unchanged.

5. Funds Transfer Regulation

As aforementioned, the anti-money laundering framework as introduced in 2015 also includes the Funds Transfer Regulation or FTR. It is interesting to see whether this regulation somehow is a useful instrument to combat the illicit use of cryptocurrencies. The FTR lays down rules on the information on payers and payees accompanying transfers of funds, in any currency, for the purposes of preventing, detecting and investigating money laundering and terrorist financing (as defined under AMLD4), where at least one of the payment service providers involved in the transfer of funds is established in the Union. Particularly, the FTR requires the payment service provider of the payer to ensure that transfers of funds are accompanied by the name of the payer, the payer's payment account number, the payer's address, official personal document number, customer identification number or date and place of birth, the name of the payee and the payee's payment account number, absent which he cannot execute any transfer of funds.

The payment service provider of the payee is required to detect missing information on the payer or the payee. Where the payment service provider of the payee becomes aware of missing or incomplete information, he must reject the transfer or ask for additional information. Furthermore, he is required to take into account missing or incomplete information on the payer or the payee as a factor when assessing whether a transfer of funds, or any related transaction, is suspicious and whether it is to be reported to the competent FIU in accordance with AMLD4. With some exceptions, the FTR applies to transfers of funds380, in any currency, which are sent or received by a payment service provider or an intermediary payment service provider established in the EU. "Funds" means banknotes and coins, scriptural money and electronic money.

Here's the rub: cryptocurrencies are none of those, and, hence out of scope. Moreover, crypto intermediaries as a rule will not be payment service providers or intermediate payment service providers in the meaning of the FTR383. This is a second reason why the FTR is not equipped to fight the illicit use of cryptocurrencies, apart from it not being designed with cryptocurrencies in mind, which is apparent from the information to be provided, especially the reference to account numbers.

6. Cash Control Regulation

As an add-on to its money laundering and terrorist financing framework, the EU enacted already in 2005 rules on the control of cash entering or leaving the Union. These rules intend to address cash movements for illicit purposes. They apply to significant movements of cash crossing the borders of the Union, i.e. cash movements equal to or above EUR 10.000 by any natural person entering or leaving the Union. Such a person must declare the cash movement, enabling customs authorities to gather information on the movements and, where appropriate, transmit that information to other authorities. In the context of the Cash Control Regulation, "cash" means: (a) bearer-negotiable instruments including monetary instruments in bearer form such as travellers cheques, negotiable instruments (including cheques, promissory notes and money orders) that are either in bearer form, endorsed without restriction, made out to a fictitious payee, or otherwise in such form that title thereto passes upon delivery and incomplete instruments (including cheques, promissory notes and money orders) signed, but with the payee's name omitted; and (b) currency (banknotes and coins that are in circulation as a medium of exchange).

Can cryptocurrencies be included in this definition? Remarkably, theoretically, there is an opening.

Coins that are in circulation as a medium of exchange are in scope. Cryptocurrencies can be seen as such coins, which is also evidenced by the AMLD5 definition of virtual currencies. However, it is clear that Cash Control Regulation is not written with the movement of cryptocurrencies in mind. It is written taking into account the physical movement of money, explaining among other things the need for declaration and the involvement of the tax authorities. Such Cryptocurrencies they are usually not physically moving: when they are moving, they are digitally moving. This makes money management the framework should never follow the movements of cryptocurrencies. From a practical point of view, a scholarly debate on the inclusion of crypto currencies in the scope of the Financial Management Act, therefore, it does not help much. One event where there can be any use is cryptocurrencies it will be stored in a portable device, such as a USB-stick, which makes the stick a type of carrier tool and this rod will be transported across the EU border. But even in this case, it is not very helpful to include it in the Cash Control Regulation program. After all I even left aside and measurement issues and data protection, seemingly ineffective - and desirable - to ensure the contents of all USB sticks or anything beyond the limits of the Union

Avoid paying taxes

The second part of this study to analyze the regulatory framework is related to tax avoidance. As already mentioned above, the EU framework for information exchange in tax matters, especially those aimed at combating tax evasion, they are not well equipped to deal with this use of tangible tax evasion funds, because you are able to share information about this, authorities must have knowledge from the beginning, which is complex, if not made impossible, by anonymity surrounding cryptocurrencies. Salvation may lie in the anti-money laundering framework and the terrorist financing framework to the extent that this framework reveals anonymity; relevant information is registered in the central area. Websites and tax authorities are able to consult and use this information; to combat tax avoiding cryptocurrency trading may work better. Is this something that can already be done under the current framework of AMLD?

First, it may be noted that the definition of "criminal activity" under AMLD4 includes tax evasion relating to direct taxes and indirect taxes, punishable by deprivation of liberty or a detention order for more than one year. Thus, the use of illegal tax revenue crime is at AMLD4 level and may include money laundering. Therefore, compulsory organizations know, suspect or have good reason to suspect that profits are due to tax evasion properly informing a competent FIU. The FIU will analyze the file and distribute the results of its analysis to competent authorities where there are reasons to suspect money laundering, related predicate cases or terrorist financing. If it is related to a border crossing file the FIUs are affected they should co-operate and exchange information obtained on a large scale it is possible. In this case, AMLD4 states that the differences between the definitions of national tax law crime will not be a barrier to the FIU's ability to exchange information or provide assistance another FIU, to the fullest extent possible under their national law.

In the context of all of this, FIUs and competent authorities should have access to beneficial resources a register of ownership, which allows them to guarantee the beneficial ownership of companies and other legal entities. This can be very helpful if these companies or other legal entities are actually set up to hide their assets profitable owners for tax avoidance purposes. Other people besides competent authorities and FIUs they cannot show legitimate interest in money laundering, terrorists finances, as well as related offenses, such as tax evasion, will also be allowed to access beneficial information information, in accordance with data protection laws, as it stands mentioned above.

Is tax administration a powerful authority that can achieve beneficial ownership? There is no definition of what constitutes a "competent authority" under AMLD4, basically which leaves it open to Member States to decide who are the most capable managers among them places are. At least in theory, this could mean that tax administration is not a skill authority. What is clear, however, is that within each Member State a competent authority must be present capable of initiating administrative or criminal proceedings against money laundering traffickers. If no, that would probably be a violation of Article 58, 2 of AMLD4, which requires Member States set up and make available to competent authorities a toolbox that allows them to do so adequate violation of penalties for national provisions introducing AMLD4. However, the fifth review of the Tax Partnership Management Order 2016 ("DAC5") removes all doubts: from 1 January 2018 the tax authorities must have access to information collected in the context of anti-money laundering and terrorist financing, which includes a register of beneficial ownership. AMLD5 recognizes this fundamental right. It clearly lists the tax authorities on the list of competent authorities should be given access to a beneficial ownership register.

Tax administration and is clearly identified in Article 49 of the revised AMLD framework, which requires Member States to ensure that the tax authorities, when operating within AMLD, have effective procedures in place be able to collaborate and connect at home about development as well implementation of anti-money laundering policies and activities and terrorist financing. In this context, it is also specified that the request for assistance between competent authorities it cannot be denied on the grounds that the application is considered to involve tax matters.

All of these redesigned submissions by DAC5 and AMLD5 strengthen the tax authorities' toolbox to continue gauntlet against tax evasion, in addition to other competent authorities may also the power of punishment in this field, as public prosecutors. The above analysis is general. What does all this mean for tax evasion through cryptocurrencies? Yes, under AMLD4 cryptocurrencies are out of place because there are no crypto players that are mandatory structures, as already analyzed above.

Therefore, no information is available internally an AMLD framework to be reached by tax authorities. So, this is not very helpful. Under AMLD5, real currency exchange platforms and fund providers monitors are compelled businesses and cryptocurrencies - in the sense of "real money" - are widely distributed. So, a little bit cryptocurrency is held by a wallet provider who is a guardian or a transaction takes place in cash exchange platform, will be the information available for tax administration, as the case may be information to tax authorities by the FIU reporting suspicious activity linked tax evasion.

Chapter Four
Investing in cryptocurrency

How to pick a cryptocurrency to invest in

Before you go ahead and buy some coins or tokens just because somebody says it's a good investment, it will pay to do some research.

First of all, it's important to understand that picking a good cryptocurrency is not like picking a good stock. A stock represents ownership in a company that creates profits for its shareholders, or at least has the potential to do so. Owning a cryptocurrency represents ownership in a digital asset with zero intrinsic value.

What makes a cryptocurrency increase or decrease in price is simple supply and demand. If there's increased demand and a limited supply increase, the price goes up. If supply becomes constrained, price goes up, and vice versa. So, when evaluating a cryptocurrency, the most important questions to answer are how the supply increases, and what will drive demand for the coin higher.

You can answer those questions by reading the white paper that a cryptocurrency team publishes to attract interest in their project. Look at the roadmap for a project and see if anything could spark an increase in demand. Research the team behind a project and see if they have the skills to execute their vision. Try to find a community of people already investing in the cryptocurrency and gauge their sentiment.

It's also important to consider how much money has already flowed into a cryptocurrency. If the market cap is already very high, there may not be much potential growth left. A high price will curb demand and increase supply as early investors look to take money off the table

How to invest in cryptocurrencies

Once you've found a cryptocurrency you think will make a good investment, it's time to start buying.

The first step is to open an account with a cryptocurrency exchange. Most stock brokers don't support trading in cryptocurrency. Coinbase (NASDAQ:COIN) is one of the most popular and beginner-friendly exchanges in the U.S. Other options include Gemini, and newer brokers such as Robinhood (NASDAQ:HOOD) and SoFi (NASDAQ:SOFI) support crypto. Just be sure the exchange you want to use also supports the cryptocurrency you want to buy.

Once you've funded your account with fiat currency, you can make an order to buy your cryptocurrency. Orders on an exchange work the same way as orders in the stock market. The exchange will match your buy order with someone making a sell order at the same price and make the trade. Once your trade is complete, the exchange will hold your cryptocurrency for you in a custodial wallet.

Buying cryptocurrency is the easy part. As a crypto investor, you have to be prepared for volatility. Crypto, in general, is more volatile than traditional asset classes such as stocks. Price swings of 10% or more in just a few hours are very common. Additionally, you should consider how much of your portfolio you ultimately want to allocate to a specific cryptocurrency and to the asset class in general. With the volatility of crypto, be sure to give yourself wide bands of acceptable allocations. If your investments fall out of those bands, be sure to rebalance.

Advantages and drawbacks to investing in cryptocurrency

Investing in cryptocurrency has a few advantages:

Diversification: The value of cryptocurrency doesn't appear to be correlated with the price of stocks, bonds, or other asset classes. That said, cryptocurrency has only existed for about a decade, so the data is limited in this regard. Theoretically, though, it makes sense that the price of crypto is unrelated to the price of traditional assets.

Return potential: Cryptocurrency has produced extremely strong returns as adoption increases. Most people agree the expected return for a sound cryptocurrency investment is greater than that for stocks.

Additional utility: Unlike stocks, some cryptocurrencies provide utility. Bitcoin (CRYPTO:BTC), for example, can be used to pay for goods and services. Other tokens may provide access to projects or discounts on a project's services.

But there are some big disadvantages for investors as well:

Limited regulation: There's limited regulation in the cryptocurrency industry, which means you don't have the same protections as you do when investing in the heavily regulated stock market. If your account gets hacked, for example, you could find your investment completely gone without any recourse. If the coin you invest in turns out to be a scam, there's nothing you can do. Furthermore, increased regulation may decrease the demand for some cryptocurrencies, adding a risk to the investment.

High volatility: The prices for cryptocurrency can swing wildly on a day-to-day basis. Such massive price swings can be hard for some investors to stomach.

Top cryptocurrencies to consider as a beginner investor

As a beginning cryptocurrency investor, you shouldn't try to find a diamond in the rough. You should get your feet wet with more established cryptocurrencies that have built-out networks to support them. That will allow you to get more familiar with the mechanics of cryptocurrency investing, as well as how it fits into your portfolio.

Bitcoin (CRYPTO:BTC) is an easy place to start. Every cryptocurrency exchange will support trading in Bitcoin. It's well-established, and you know what you're getting with Bitcoin. It's nothing fancy, just digital cash, but it has a first-mover advantage that had made it widely adopted. That gives Bitcoin a competitive advantage when it comes to being actually usable as a medium of exchange.

Ether (CRYPTO:ETH) is also a good choice for beginner investors. Ethereum's technology is behind most DeFi projects, which use the Ethereum blockchain to execute smart contracts and provide financial services without a central authority. Anytime a user wants to write a smart contract to the blockchain, they'll have to pay Ether to do so. Increased acceptance of DeFi applications will lead to greater Ether demand.

The third option for beginner investors is Cardano (CRYPTO: ADA). Cardano offers another Ethereum solution designed to save more power by using a stack proof proof system to validate blocks in the blockchain. Therefore, it currently has a much lower transaction costs than Ethereum. Additionally, Cardano has a strong cap on the full supply of token like Bitcoin. That means the supply may be difficult in the future, which will increase the price.

Making money by investing in cryptocurrencies

Investing in crypto requires you to do your research and be confident enough in your investment to stick to what is sure to be a bad trip. If you can do that, the payment may be worth it as the expected return is higher than most other categories of assets.

Conclusion

When it was first introduced, Bitcoin was intended to be a daily trading platform, making it possible to buy everything from a cup of coffee to a computer or even large ticket items like houses. That really did not happen and, while the number of cryptocurrency institutions is growing, large-scale transactions involved are rare. However, it is possible to purchase a variety of products on e-commerce websites using crypto. Here are some examples:

Technology and e-commerce sites:

A few companies that sell technology products adopt crypto on their websites, such as newgg.com, AT&T, and Microsoft. Overstock, an e-commerce platform, was one of the first to adopt Bitcoin.

Shopify, Rakuten, and Home Depot also welcome you.

Luxury goods:

Some elite merchants accept crypto as a payment method. For example, Bitdials online retailers offer Rolex, Patek Philippe, and other high-end watches as a return to Bitcoin.

Vehicles:

Some car dealers - from large market companies to high-end retailers - are already accepting crypto currency as payment.

Insurance:

In April 2021, Swiss insurance AXA announced that it had begun accepting Bitcoin as a payment method for all of its insurance lines other than life insurance (due to regulatory issues). Premier Shield Insurance, which sells home and car insurance policies in the US, also accepts Bitcoin for premium payments.

If you want to use cryptocurrency on a non-accepting merchant, you can use a cryptocurrency debit card, such as BitPay in the US.

Cryptocurrency fraud and cryptocurrency scams

Unfortunately, cryptocurrency crime is on the rise. Cryptocurrency scams include:

Fake websites: Fake sites include false testimonials and crypto jargon that promises huge, guaranteed returns, as long as you continue to invest.

Virtual Ponzi schemes: Cryptocurrency criminals promote non-existent digital investment opportunities and create huge profit scams by paying older investors with the money of new investors. One scam operation, BitClub Network, raised more than $ 700 million before the perpetrators were charged in December 2019.

"Famous" recommendations: Fraudsters pretend to be online as billionaires or well-known brands that promise to double your investment with real money but instead steal what you post. They may also use messaging apps or chat rooms to start rumors that a well-known businessman is sponsoring some crypto currency. Once they have encouraged investors to buy and raise the price, fraudsters sell their stake, and the money goes down in value.

Romance scams: The FBI warns of online dating scams, in which scammers entice people they meet on dating sites or on social media to invest or trade for tangible amounts. The FBI's Internet Crime Complaint Center has reported more than 1,800 crypto-based love scams in the first seven months of 2021, with losses amounting to $ 133 million.

Otherwise, fraudulent entities may appear to be legitimate money changers or to establish fraudulent transactions in order to defraud people. Another crypto scam involves fraudulent trading transactions for individual retirement accounts in cryptocurrencies. Then there is direct cryptocurrency theft, where criminals break into digital wallets where people keep their visible money in order to steal it.

Is cryptocurrency safe?

Cryptocurrencies are usually created using blockchain technology. Blockchain describes how transactions are recorded on "blocks" and time stamped. It is a complex, technical process, but the result is a digital cryptocurrency transaction book that is difficult for criminals to compromise.

In addition, the transaction requires a two-factor authentication process. For example, you may be asked to enter a username and password to start the process. Then, you may need to enter a verification code sent in text on your own cell phone.

While securities exist, that does not mean that cryptocurrencies cannot be stolen. Several high-cost hacks have cost the implementation of cryptocurrency very much. The hackers beat Coincheck to $ 534 million and BitGrail for $ 195 million, making them the two biggest cryptocurrency criminals of 2018.

Unlike government subsidies, the amount of cash flows is entirely driven by supply and demand. This can create unusual volatility that generates huge profits for investors or huge losses. And cryptocurrency investments are subject to much less regulatory protection than traditional financial products such as stocks, bonds, and joint ventures.

Four tips for investing in cryptocurrency safely

According to Consumer Reports, all investments are risky, but some experts consider cryptocurrency as one of the risky investment options out there. If you are planning to invest in cryptocurrencies, these tips can help you make informed decisions.

Research interviews:

Before investing, learn about cryptocurrency trading. It is estimated that there are over 500 trading options. Do your research, read reviews, and talk to more experienced investors before moving on.

Know how to save your digital money:

If you buy cryptocurrency, you should keep it. You can save it in exchange or in a digital wallet. Although there are different types of wallets, each has its own advantages, technical requirements, and security. As an exchange, you should research your storage options before investing.

Divide your investment:

Variety is the key to any good investment strategy, and this is especially true if you are investing in cryptocurrency. Do not invest all your money in

Bitcoin, for example, because that is the name you know. There are thousands of options, and it is best to spread your investment in a few currencies.

Configure flexibility:

The cryptocurrency market is highly volatile, so be prepared for ups and downs. You will see dramatic swings in prices. If your investment portfolio or mental wellbeing can't handle that, cryptocurrency might not be a wise choice for you.

Cryptocurrency is all the rage right now, but remember, it is still in its relative infancy and is considered highly speculative. Investing in something new comes with challenges, so be prepared. If you plan to participate, do your research, and invest conservatively to start.

One of the best ways you can stay safe online is by using a comprehensive antivirus. Kaspersky Internet Security defends you from malware infections, spyware, data theft and protects your online payments using bank-grade encryption.

www.ingramcontent.com/pod-product-compliance
Lightning Source LLC
Chambersburg PA
CBHW052314220526
45472CB00001B/113